EXPRESSION AND MEANING

Studies in the Theory of Speech Acts

FOR THOMAS AND MARK

EXPRESSION AND MEANING

Studies in the Theory of Speech Acts

JOHN R. SEARLE

Professor of Philosophy
University of California, Berkeley

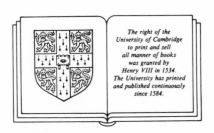

The right of the
University of Cambridge
to print and sell
all manner of books
was granted by
Henry VIII in 1534.
The University has printed
and published continuously
since 1584.

CAMBRIDGE UNIVERSITY PRESS

Cambridge
New York   Port Chester
Melbourne   Sydney

Published by the Press Syndicate of the University of Cambridge
The Pitt Building, Trumpington Street, Cambridge CB2 1RP
32 East 57th Street, New York, NY 10022, USA
10 Stamford Road, Oakleigh, Melbourne 3166, Australia

© Cambridge University Press 1979

First published 1979
Reprinted 1981
First paperback edition 1985
Reprinted 1986 (twice), 1989

Printed in the United States of America

Library of Congress Cataloging in Publication Data
Searle, John R.
Expression and meaning.
Bibliography: p.
Includes index.
I. Speech acts (Linguistics) I. Title.
P95.55.S4   401   79–12271
ISBN 0 521 22901 4 hard covers
ISBN 0 521 31393 7 paperback

CONTENTS

ACKNOWLEDGEMENTS

I am grateful to the John Simon Guggenheim Memorial Foundation and to the University of California, Berkeley, Humanities Institute for grants which enabled me to work on these essays and other related topics. I have benefited enormously from discussions of these questions with students, colleagues and friends, and I am especially grateful to Hubert Dreyfus. Thanks are also due to Susan Eason for work on the index and Savannah Ross for organizing the typing. Most of all I wish to thank my wife, Dagmar Searle, for her constant help and advice.

INTRODUCTION

These essays represent a continuation of a line of research begun in *Speech Acts* (Searle, 1969). Most of them were originally projected as chapters of a larger work in which discussions of some of the outstanding problems of speech act theory – for example, metaphor, fiction, indirect speech acts, and a classification of types of speech acts – were to have been embedded in a general theory of meaning, in which I hoped to show in what ways the philosophy of language was based on the philosophy of mind, and in particular how certain features of speech acts were based on the Intentionality of the mind. The original chapter on Intentionality however has now grown into a book length manuscript of its own, and when the Intentionalistic tail outgrew the linguistic dog it seemed a better idea to publish these studies as a separate volume. This book then is not intended as a collection of unrelated essays, and my main aim in this introduction is to say something about how they are related.

One of the most obvious questions in any philosophy of language is: how many ways of using language are there? Wittgenstein thought the question unanswerable by any finite list of categories. "But how many kinds of sentence are there? ... There are *countless* [unzählige] kinds" (1953, para. 23). But this rather skeptical conclusion ought to arouse our suspicions. No one I suppose would say that there are countless kinds of economic systems or marital arrangements or sorts of political parties; why should language be more taxonomically recalcitrant than any other aspect of human social life? I argue in the first essay that if we take the illocutionary act (that is, the full blown illocutionary act with its illocutionary force and propositional content) as the unit of analysis, as I believe we should for quite independent reasons (see Searle, 1969, Ch. 1), then we find there are five general ways of using language, five general categories of illocutionary acts. We tell people how things are (Assertives),[1] we try to get them to do things (Directives), we commit ourselves to doing things (Commissives), we express our feelings and attitudes (Expressives), and we bring about changes in the world through our utterances (Declarations).

The method I use in this essay is in a sense empirical. I simply look at uses of language and find these five types of illocutionary point, and when I examine actual discourse I find, or at least claim, that utterances can be classified under these headings. But any philosopher is bound to feel that where there are categories there ought to be a transcendental deduction of the categories, that is, there ought to be some theoretical explanation as to why language provides us with these and with only these.[2] The justification of these categories in terms of the nature of the mind has to wait for the next book. But one problem which immediately arises for this book is that one and the same utterance will often fit into more than one category. Suppose I say to you, for example, "Sir, you are standing on my foot." Now in most contexts when I make a statement of that sort I am making not only an Assertive, but I am also indirectly requesting and perhaps even ordering you to get off my foot. Thus the Assertive utterance is also an indirect Directive. How does such an utterance work, that is, how do both speaker and hearer go so effortlessly from the literal Assertive sentence meaning to the implied indirect Directive utterance meaning? The second essay, "Indirect speech acts", opens what is perhaps the main theme of this collection: the relations between literal sentence meaning and speaker's utterance meaning, where

---

[1] In the original publication I used the term "Representative", but I now prefer "Assertive" since any speech act with a propositional content is in some sense a representation.

[2] I do not of course claim that every one of the world's two thousand or so natural languages has the syntactical devices for expressing all five types. For all I know there may be languages that have not evolved syntactical devices for, e.g., Commissives.

utterance meaning differs from the literal meaning of the expression uttered. In the special case of indirect speech acts, the speaker means what he says but he also means something more, and the aim of chapter 2 is to articulate the principles on which this sort of implied communication is possible.

Perhaps the chief methodological conclusion to be derived from this essay as far as contemporary linguistics is concerned is that we do not need to postulate either alternative deep structures or an extra set of conversational postulates to account for these cases, and discussion of these methodological morals is resumed more explicitly in the last essay. Another more general methodological lesson from the first two essays is that we must not confuse an analysis of illocutionary verbs with an analysis of illocutionary acts. There are many illocutionary verbs that are not restricted as to illocutionary point, that is, they can take a large range of illocutionary points, and thus they do not genuinely name an illocutionary force. "Announce", "hint", and "insinuate", for example, do not name types of illocutionary acts, but rather the style or manner in which a rather large range of types can be performed. I believe the single most common mistake in speech act theory is the confusion between features of illocutionary verbs and illocutionary acts. Several taxonomies I have seen, including Austin's (1962), confuse a taxonomy of illocutionary acts with one of illocutionary verbs; and more recently some philosophers (e.g. Holdcroft, 1978) erroneously conclude from the fact that some verbs such as "hint" name a deliberately inexplicit manner of performing a speech act that some types of meaning are therefore inherently inexpressible; and thus they erroneously conclude that they have refuted the principle of expressibility, the principle that whatever can be meant can be said. But, for example, hinting is not part of meaning in the sense that hinting is neither part of illocutionary force nor propositional content. Illocutionary acts are, so to speak, natural conceptual kinds, and we should no more suppose that our ordinary language verbs carve the conceptual field of illocutions at its semantic joints than we would suppose that our ordinary language expressions for naming and describing plants and animals correspond exactly to the natural biological kinds.

Chapter 2, Indirect speech acts, opens the discussions of the relation between literal sentence meaning and intended speaker's utterance meaning; and these relations are further explored in chapters 3 and 4 on fiction and metaphor. In the sense in which the first essay lists types of speech acts, neither fiction nor metaphor is a separate type of speech act; these categories cut the linguistic pie from an altogether different direction. From the point of view of the philosophy of language the problem of fiction is: how can the speaker utter a sentence with a certain meaning (whether literal or not) and yet not be committed to the truth conditions carried by that meaning? How for example does fictional discourse differ from lies? And from the same point of view the chief problem of metaphor is how can the speaker systematically mean and communicate something quite different from what the expressions he utters mean? How do we get from literal expression meaning to metaphorical utterance meaning? In both chapters I try to give a systematic account of the principles according to which these types of language use really work, but the results are quite different in the two cases. Fiction I think is a rather easy problem (at least by the usual standards of philosophical intractability), but metaphor is hard, and though I feel confident that my misgivings about both the "comparison" theories of metaphor and their "interactionist" rivals are justified, I am equally confident that my own account is at best incomplete because I have in all likelihood not stated all of the principles involved in the production and comprehension of metaphor; and perhaps the most interesting of my principles, number 4, is not so much a "principle" as simply a statement that there are sets of associations, many of them psychologically grounded, which enable certain types of metaphors to work, even though they are not underlain by any literal similarities or other principles of association.

The first four chapters take the notion of the literal meaning of expressions, whether words or sentences, for granted; but the assumptions behind the current philosophical and linguistic employment of this notion are scrutinized in chapter 5, "Literal meaning". I argue against the theory that the literal meaning of a sentence can be construed as the meaning that it has apart from any context whatever, the meaning that it has in the so called "null context". Against this view I contend that the notion of literal meaning only has application against a background of assumptions and practices which are not themselves represented as part of literal meaning. I further argue that this conclusion does not in any way weaken the system of distinctions that revolve around the distinction between speaker meaning and literal sentence meaning – the distinctions between literal and metaphorical utterances, between fiction and nonfiction, and between direct and indirect speech acts. Given the background of practices and assumptions which makes communication possible at all, each of these distinctions is necessary to an accurate account of the functioning of language. And though, of course, for each distinction there are many borderline cases, the principles of the distinction, principles which it is one of the chief aims of this book to articulate, can be made reasonably clear.

Since Frege, reference has been regarded as the central problem in the philosophy of language; and by reference I mean not predication, or truth, or extension but *reference*, the relation between such expressions as definite descriptions and proper names on the one hand, and the things they are used to refer to on the other. I now think it was a mistake to take this as the central problem in the philosophy of language, because we will not get an adequate theory of linguistic reference until we can show how such a theory is part of a general theory of Intentionality, a theory of how the mind is related to objects in the world in general. But in the hope that some fairly well defined problems within the theory of reference can be attacked with tools available at present, I turn to some of the problems surrounding definite descriptions in chapter 6, "Referential and attributive". According to a currently influential view there is a fundamental linguistic distinction between the referential and the attributive use of definite descriptions, a difference so fundamental that it gives different truth conditions for utterances depending on which use is in question. I argue that this distinction is misconceived, and in fact the linguistic data are instances of the general distinction used throughout this book between the meaning of the expressions that a speaker utters and his intended meaning, where, as in this case, his intended meaning may include the literal meaning of the expressions he utters but is not exhausted by that literal meaning.

In the final essay, "Speech acts and recent linguistics", I try to make fully explicit some of the methodological implications of the earlier essays for contemporary linguistics. I argue that both the practice of postulating additional syntactic deep structures to account for speech act phenomena, as exemplified most prominently by Ross's (1970) performative deletion analysis of all sentences of a natural language such as English, and the practice of postulating extra rules or conversational postulates, as exemplified by Gordon and Lakoff's (1971) conversational postulate analysis of indirect speech acts, are mistaken; and both, in spite of their apparently quite different formal mechanisms, make the same mistake of hypostatizing an extra and unnecessary apparatus when we already have independently motivated analytic principles that are adequate and sufficient to account for the data.

In the past decade, since the publication of *Speech Acts*, I have been confronted with three sets of problems in the philosophy of language. First there are specific problems that arise within the existing paradigm. Second there is the problem of grounding the whole theory in the philosophy of mind, and third there is the challenge of trying to provide an adequate formalization of the theory using the resources of modern logic, particularly set theory. This book is entirely addressed to the first of these problems. I intend to publish an account of the second in *Intentionality* (Cambridge University Press, forthcoming), and I am working with Daniel Vanderveken on the third in an exploration of the foundations of illocutionary logic.

ORIGINS OF THE ESSAYS

Almost all of the material in this volume was first presented in lectures and seminars in Berkeley and in invited lectures and conferences at various other universities. "A taxonomy of illocutionary acts" was originally presented as a Forum Lecture to the Summer Linguistics Institute in Buffalo, NY in 1971 and was subsequently the topic of various lectures in Europe and the US. It first appeared in print in *Language, Mind, and Knowledge, Minnesota Studies in the Philosophy of Science*, Vol. VII, ed. Keith Gunderson, Univ. of Minnesota Press, 1975, pp. 344–69. It also appeared in the same year in the journal *Language and Society*, under the title "A Classification of Illocutionary Acts".

"Indirect speech acts" first appeared in *Syntax and Semantics Vol. 3, Speech Acts*, Peter Cole and Jerry Morgan (eds.), Academic Press 1975. It was also the subject of a Summer Linguistics Institute Forum lecture, in Amherst, 1974.

"Literal meaning" was first presented in part at the Speech Act Working Group of the International Linguistics Congress in Vienna in Summer of 1977 and also at the Speech Acts Conference in Döbögokö, Hungary, immediately following the Congress in Vienna. It was first published in *Erkenntnis*, Vol. 13, No. 1, July 1978, pp. 207–24.

"The logical status of fictional discourse" was first published in *New Literary History* 1974–5, Vol. VI, pp. 319–32, having been the topic of lectures at various universities including Minnesota, Virginia and Louvain.

"Metaphor" was originally presented at a conference on that subject at the University of Illinois in 1977. It is forthcoming in the proceedings of the conference *Metaphor and thought*, Andrew Ortony (ed.), Cambridge Univ. Press, 1979.

"Referential and attributive" was originally written for a special issue of *The Monist* on the subject of Reference and Truth. Forthcoming, 1979.

"Speech acts and recent linguistics" was the keynote address at the New York Academy of Science Conference on Developmental Linguistics and Communication Disorders. It was published in the *Annals* of the Academy, 1975, Vol. 263, Doris Aaronson and Robert W. Rieber (eds.), pp. 27–38.

Chapter 1

A TAXONOMY OF ILLOCUTIONARY ACTS

I. INTRODUCTION

The primary purpose of this paper is to develop a reasoned classification of illocutionary acts into certain basic categories or types. It is to answer the question: How many kinds of illocutionary acts are there?

Since any such attempt to develop a taxonomy must take into account Austin's classification of illocutionary acts into his five basic categories of verdictive, expositive, exercitive, behabitive, and commissive, a second purpose of this paper is to assess Austin's classification to show in what respects it is adequate and in what respects inadequate. Furthermore, since basic semantic differences are likely to have syntactical consequences, a third purpose of this paper is to show how these different basic illocutionary types are realized in the syntax of a natural language such as English.

In what follows, I shall presuppose a familiarity with the general pattern of analysis of illocutionary acts offered in such works as *How to Do Things with Words* (Austin, 1962), *Speech Acts* (Searle, 1969), and "Austin on Locutionary and Illocutionary Acts" (Searle, 1968). In particular, I shall presuppose a distinction between the illocutionary force of an utterance and its propositional content as symbolized

$$F(p)$$

The aim of this paper then is to classify the different types of F.

II. DIFFERENT TYPES OF DIFFERENCES BETWEEN DIFFERENT TYPES OF ILLOCUTIONARY ACTS

Any taxonomical effort of this sort presupposes criteria for distinguishing one (kind of) illocutionary act from another.

What are the criteria by which we can tell that of three actual utterances one is a report, one a prediction and one a promise? In order to develop higher order genera, we must first know how the species *promise, prediction, report*, etc., differ from one another. When one attempts to answer that question one discovers that there are several quite different principles of distinction; that is, there are different kinds of differences that enable us to say that the force of this utterance is different from the force of that utterance. For this reason the metaphor of force in the expression "illocutionary force" is misleading since it suggests that different illocutionary forces occupy different positions on a single continuum of force. What is actually the case is that there are several distinct criss-crossing continua. A related source of confusion is that we are inclined to confuse illocutionary verbs with types of illocutionary acts. We are inclined, for example, to think that where we have two nonsynonymous illocutionary verbs they must necessarily mark two different kinds of illocutionary acts. In what follows, I shall try to keep a clear distinction between illocutionary verbs and illocutionary acts. Illocutions are a part of language as opposed to particular languages. Illocutionary verbs are always part of a particular language: French, German, English, or whatnot. Differences in illocutionary verbs are a good guide but by no means a sure guide to differences in illocutionary acts.

It seems to me there are (at least) twelve significant dimensions of variation in which illocutionary acts differ one from another and I shall – all too briskly – list them:

1. *Differences in the point (or purpose) of the (type of) act.* The point or purpose of an order can be specified by saying that it is an attempt to get the hearer to do something. The point or purpose of a description is that it is a representation (true or false, accurate or inaccurate) of how something is. The point or purpose of a promise is that it is an undertaking of an obligation by the speaker to do something. These differences correspond to the essential conditions in my analysis of illocutionary acts in chapter 3 of *Speech Acts* (Searle, 1969). Ultimately, I believe, essential conditions form the best basis for a taxonomy, as I shall attempt to show. It is important to

notice that the terminology of "point" or "purpose" is not meant to imply, nor is it based on the view, that every illocutionary act has a definitionally associated perlocutionary intent. For many, perhaps most, of the most important illocutionary acts, there is no essential perlocutionary intent associated by definition with the corresponding verb, e.g. statements and promises are not by definition attempts to produce perlocutionary effects in hearers.

The point or purpose of a type of illocution I shall call its *illocutionary point*. Illocutionary point is part of but not the same as illocutionary force. Thus, e.g., the illocutionary point of requests is the same as that of commands: both are attempts to get hearers to do something. But the illocutionary forces are clearly different. In general, one can say that the notion of illocutionary force is the resultant of several elements of which illocutionary point is only one, though, I believe, the most important one.

2. *Differences in the direction of fit between words and the world.* Some illocutions have as part of their illocutionary point to get the words (more strictly, their propositional content) to match the world, others to get the world to match the words. Assertions are in the former category, promises and requests are in the latter. The best illustration of this distinction I know of is provided by Elizabeth Anscombe (1957). Suppose a man goes to the supermarket with a shopping list given him by his wife on which are written the words "beans, butter, bacon, and bread". Suppose as he goes around with his shopping cart selecting these items, he is followed by a detective who writes down everything he takes. As they emerge from the store both shopper and detective will have identical lists. But the function of the two lists will be quite different. In the case of the shopper's list, the purpose of the list is, so to speak, to get the world to match the words; the man is supposed to make his actions fit the list. In the case of the detective, the purpose of the list is to make the words match the world; the man is supposed to make the list fit the actions of the shopper. This can be further demonstrated by observing the role of "mistake" in the two cases. If the

3

detective gets home and suddenly realizes that the man bought pork chops instead of bacon, he can simply erase the word "bacon" and write "pork chops". But if the shopper gets home and his wife points out he has bought pork chops when he should have bought bacon he cannot correct the mistake by erasing "bacon" from the list and writing "pork chops".

In these examples the list provides the propositional content of the illocution and the illocutionary force determines how that content is supposed to relate to the world. I propose to call this difference a difference in *direction of fit*. The detective's list has the *word-to-world* direction of fit (as do statements, descriptions, assertions, and explanations); the shopper's list has the *world-to-word* direction of fit (as do requests, commands, vows, promises). I represent the word-to-world direction of fit with a downward arrow thus ↓ and the world-to-word direction of fit with an upward arrow thus ↑. Direction of fit is always a consequence of illocutionary point. It would be very elegant if we could build our taxonomy entirely around this distinction in direction of fit, but though it will figure largely in our taxonomy, I am unable to make it the entire basis of the distinctions.

3. *Differences in expressed psychological states.* A man who states, explains, asserts or claims that *p expresses the belief that p*; a man who promises, vows, threatens or pledges to do *a expresses an intention to do a*; a man who orders, commands, requests H to do *A expresses a desire (want, wish) that H do A*; a man who apologizes for doing *A expresses regret at having done A*; etc. In general, in the performance of any illocutionary act with a propositional content, the speaker expresses some attitude, state, etc., to that propositional content. Notice that this holds even if he is insincere, even if he does not have the belief, desire, intention, regret or pleasure which he expresses, he nonetheless expresses a belief, desire, intention, regret or pleasure in the performance of the speech act. This fact is marked linguistically by the fact that it is linguistically unacceptable (though not self-contradictory) to conjoin the explicit performative verb with the denial of the expressed

psychological state. Thus one cannot say "I state that *p* but do not believe that *p*", "I promise that *p* but I do not intend that *p*", etc. Notice that this only holds in the first person performative use. One can say, "He stated that *p* but didn't really believe that *p*", "I promised that *p* but did not really intend to do it", etc. The psychological state expressed in the performance of the illocutionary act is the *sincerity condition* of the act, as analyzed in *Speech Acts*, Ch. 3.

If one tries to do a classification of illocutionary acts based entirely on differently expressed psychological states (differences in the sincerity condition) one can get quite a long way. Thus, *belief* collects not only statements, assertions, remarks and explanations, but also postulations, declarations, deductions and arguments. *Intention* will collect promises, vows, threats and pledges. *Desire* or *want* will collect requests, orders, commands, askings, prayers, pleadings, beggings and entreaties. *Pleasure* doesn't collect quite so many – congratulations, felicitations, welcomes and a few others.

In what follows, I shall symbolize the expressed psychological state with the capitalized initial letters of the corresponding verb, thus *B* for believe, *W* for want, *I* for intend, etc.

These three dimensions – illocutionary point, direction of fit, and sincerity condition – seem to me the most important, and I will build most of my taxonomy around them, but there are several others that need remarking.

4. *Differences in the force or strength with which the illocutionary point is presented.* Both, "I suggest we go to the movies" and "I insist that we go to the movies" have the same illocutionary point, but it is presented with different strengths. Analogously with "I solemnly swear that Bill stole the money" and "I guess Bill stole the money". Along the same dimension of illocutionary point or purpose there may be varying degrees of strength or commitment.

5. *Differences in the status or position of the speaker and hearer as these bear on the illocutionary force of the utterance.* If the general asks the private to clean up the room, that is in all likelihood a command or an order. If the private asks the general to clean

up the room, that is likely to be a suggestion or proposal or request but not an order or command. This feature corresponds to one of the preparatory conditions in my analysis in *Speech Acts*, chapter 3.

6. *Differences in the way the utterance relates to the interests of the speaker and the hearer.* Consider, for example, the differences between boasts and laments, between congratulations and condolences. In these two pairs, one hears the difference as being between what is or is not in the interests of the speaker and hearer respectively. This feature is another type of preparatory condition according to the analysis in *Speech Acts*.

7. *Differences in relations to the rest of the discourse.* Some performative expressions serve to relate the utterance to the rest of the discourse (and also to the surrounding context). Consider, e.g., "I reply", "I deduce", "I conclude", and "I object". These expressions serve to relate utterances to other utterances and to the surrounding context. The features they mark seem mostly to involve utterances within the class of statements. In addition to simply stating a proposition, one may state it by way of objecting to what someone else has said, by way of replying to an earlier point, by way of deducing it from certain evidentiary premises, etc. "However", "moreover" and "therefore" also perform these discourse relating functions.

8. *Differences in propositional content that are determined by illocutionary force indicating devices.* The differences, for example, between a report and a prediction involve the fact that a prediction must be about the future whereas a report can be about the past or present. These differences correspond to differences in propositional content conditions as explained in *Speech Acts*.

9. *Differences between those acts that must always be speech acts, and those that can be, but need not be performed as speech acts.* For example, one may classify things by saying "I classify this as an *A* and this as a *B*". But, one need not say anything at all in order to be classifying; one may simply throw all the *A*s in the *A* box and all the *B*s in the *B* box. Similarly with estimate, diagnose and conclude. I may make estimates, give diagnoses and draw conclusions in saying "I estimate", "I diagnose",

6

and "I conclude", but in order to estimate, diagnose or conclude it is not necessary to say anything at all. I may simply stand before a building and estimate its height, silently diagnose you as a marginal schizophrenic, or conclude that the man sitting next to me is quite drunk. In these cases, no speech act, not even an internal speech act, is necessary.

10. *Differences between those acts that require extra-linguistic institutions for their performance and those that do not.* There are a large number of illocutionary acts that require an extra-linguistic institution, and generally, a special position by the speaker and the hearer within that institution in order for the act to be performed. Thus, in order to bless, excommunicate, christen, pronounce guilty, call the base runner out, bid three no-trumps, or declare war, it is not sufficient for any old speaker to say to any old hearer "I bless", "I excommunicate", etc. One must have a position within an extra-linguistic institution. Austin sometimes talks as if he thought all illocutionary acts were like this, but plainly they are not. In order to make a statement that it is raining or promise to come and see you, I need only obey the rules of language. No extra-linguistic institutions are required. This feature of certain speech acts, that they require extra-linguistic institutions, needs to be distinguished from feature 5, the requirement of certain illocutionary acts that the speaker and possibly the hearer as well have a certain status. Extra-linguistic institutions often confer status in a way relevant to illocutionary force, but not all differences of status derive from institutions. Thus, an armed robber in virtue of his possession of a gun may *order* as opposed to, e.g., request, entreat, or implore victims to raise their hands. But his status here does not derive from a position within an institution but from his possession of a weapon.

11. *Differences between those acts where the corresponding illocutionary verb has a performative use and those where it does not.* Most illocutionary verbs have performative uses – e.g. "state", "promise", "order", "conclude". But one cannot perform acts of, e.g., boasting or threatening, by saying "I hereby boast", or "I hereby threaten". Not all illocutionary verbs are performative verbs.

A taxonomy of illocutionary acts

12. Differences in the style of performance of the illocutionary act. Some illocutionary verbs serve to mark what we might call the special *style* in which an illocutionary act is performed. Thus, the difference between, for example, announcing and confiding need not involve any difference in illocutionary point or propositional content but only in the *style* of performance of the illocutionary act.

III. WEAKNESSES IN AUSTIN'S TAXONOMY

Austin advances his five categories very tentatively, more as a basis for discussion than as a set of established results. "I am not", he says, "putting any of this forward as in the very least definitive" (Austin, 1962, p. 151). I think they form an excellent basis for discussion but I also think that the taxonomy needs to be seriously revised because it contains several weaknesses. Here are Austin's five categories:

Verdictives. These "consist in the delivering of a finding, official or unofficial, upon evidence or reasons as to value or fact so far as these are distinguishable". Examples of verbs in this class are: acquit, hold, calculate, describe, analyze, estimate, date, rank, assess, and characterize.

Exercitives. One of these "is the giving of a decision in favor of or against a certain course of action or advocacy of it . . .", "a decision that something is to be so, as distinct from a judgment that it is so". Some examples are: order, command, direct, plead, beg, recommend, entreat and advise. Request is also an obvious example, but Austin does not list it. As well as the above, Austin also lists: appoint, dismiss, nominate, veto, declare closed, declare open, as well as announce, warn, proclaim, and give.

Commissives. "The whole point of a commissive," Austin tells us, "is to commit the speaker to a certain course of action." Some of the obvious examples are: promise, vow, pledge, covenant, contract, guarantee, embrace, and swear.

Expositives "are used in acts of exposition involving the expounding of views, the conducting of arguments and the clarifying of usages and references". Austin gives many examples of these, among which are: affirm, deny, emphasize, illustrate, answer, report, accept, object to, concede, describe, class, identify and call.

Behabitives. This class, with which Austin was very dissatisfied ("a shocker", he called it), "includes the notion of reaction to other people's behaviour and fortunes and of attitudes and expressions of attitudes to someone else's past conduct or imminent conduct."

Among the examples Austin lists are: apologize, thank, deplore, commiserate, congratulate, felicitate, welcome, applaud, criticize, bless, curse, toast and drink. But also, curiously: dare, defy, protest, and challenge.

The first thing to notice about these lists is that they are not classifications of illocutionary acts but of English illocutionary verbs. Austin seems to assume that a classification of different verbs is *eo ipso* a classification of kinds of illocutionary acts, that any two non-synonymous verbs must mark different illocutionary acts. But there is no reason to suppose that this is the case. As we shall see, some verbs, for example, mark the manner in which an illocutionary act is performed, e.g. "announce". One may announce orders, promises and reports, but announcing is not on all fours with ordering, promising and reporting. Announcing, to anticipate a bit, is not the name of a type of illocutionary act, but of the way in which some illocutionary act is performed. An announcement is never just an announcement. It must also be a statement, order, etc.

Even granting that the lists are of illocutionary verbs and not necessarily of different illocutionary acts, it seems to me, one can level the following criticisms against it.

1. First, a minor cavil, but one worth noting. Not all of the verbs listed are even illocutionary verbs. For example, "sympathize", "regard as", "mean to", "intend", and "shall". Take, "intend": it is clearly not performative. Saying, "I intend" is not intending; nor in the third person does it name an illocutionary act: "He intended . . ." does not report a speech act. Of course there is an illocutionary act of *expressing an intention*, but the illocutionary verb phrase is: "express an intention", not "intend". Intending is never a speech act; expressing an intention usually, but not always, is.

9

2. The most important weakness of the taxonomy is simply this. There is no clear or consistent principle or set of principles on the basis of which the taxonomy is constructed. Only in the case of Commissives has Austin clearly and unambiguously used illocutionary point as the basis of the definition of a category. Expositives, insofar as the characterization is clear, seem to be defined in terms of discourse relations (my feature 7). Exercitives seem to be at least partly defined in terms of the exercise of authority. Both considerations of status (my feature 5 above) as well as institutional considerations (my feature 10) are lurking in it. Behabitives do not seem to me at all well defined (as Austin, I am sure, would have agreed) but it seems to involve notions of what is good or bad for the speaker and hearer (my feature 6) as well as expressions of attitudes (my feature 3).

3. Because there is no clear principle of classification and because there is a persistent confusion between illocutionary acts and illocutionary verbs, there is a great deal of overlap from one category to another and a great deal of heterogeneity within some of the categories. The problem is not that there are borderline cases – any taxonomy that deals with the real world is likely to come up with borderline cases – nor is it merely that a few unusual cases will have the defining characteristics of more than one category, rather a very large number of verbs find themselves smack in the middle of two competing categories because the principles of classification are unsystematic. Consider, for example, the verb "describe", a very important verb in anybody's theory of speech acts. Austin lists it as both a verdictive and an expositive. Given his definitions, it is easy to see why: describing can be both the delivering of a finding and an act of exposition. But then any "act of exposition involving the expounding of views" could also in his rather special sense be "the delivering of a finding, official or unofficial, upon evidence or reasons". And indeed, a look at his list of expositives (pp. 161–2) is sufficient to show that most of his verbs fit his definition of verdictives as well as does "describe". Consider "affirm", "deny", "state", "class", "identify", "conclude", and "deduce". All of these are listed

as expositives, but they could just as easily have been listed as verdictives. The few cases which are clearly not verdictives are cases where the meaning of the verb has purely to do with discourse relations, e.g. "begin by", "turn to", or where there is no question of evidence or reasons, e.g. "postulate", "neglect", "call", and "define". But then that is really not sufficient to warrant a separate category, especially since many of these – "begin by", "turn to", "neglect", are not names of illocutionary acts at all.

4. Not only is there too much overlap from one category to the next, but within some of the categories there are quite distinct kinds of verbs. Thus Austin lists "dare", "defy" and "challenge", alongside "thank", "apologize", "deplore", and "welcome" as behabitives. But "dare", "defy" and "challenge" have to do with the hearer's subsequent actions, they belong with "order", "command" and "forbid" both on syntactical and semantic grounds, as I shall argue later. But when we look for the family that includes "order", "command" and "urge", we find these are listed as exercitives alongside "veto", "hire" and "demote". But these, again as I shall argue later, are in two quite distinct categories.

5. Related to these objections is the further difficulty that not all of the verbs listed within the classes really satisfy the definitions given, even if we take the definitions in the rather loose and suggestive manner that Austin clearly intends. Thus "nominate", "appoint" and "excommunicate" are not "giving of a decision in favour of or against a certain course of action", much less are they "advocating" it. Rather they are, as Austin himself might have said, *performances* of these actions, not *advocacies* of anything. That is, in the sense in which we might agree that ordering, commanding and urging someone to do something are all cases of *advocating* that he do it, we cannot also agree that nominating or appointing is also advocating. When I appoint you chairman, I don't advocate that you be or become chairman; I *make* you chairman.

In sum, there are (at least) six related difficulties with Austin's taxonomy; in ascending order of importance: there is a persistent confusion between verbs and acts, not all the verbs are illocutionary verbs, there is too much overlap of the categories, too much heterogeneity within the categories, many of the verbs listed in the categories don't satisfy the definition given for the category and, most important, there is no consistent principle of classification.

I don't believe I have fully substantiated all six of these charges and I will not attempt to do so within the confines of this paper, which has other aims. I believe, however, that my doubts about Austin's taxonomy will have greater clarity and force after I have presented an alternative. What I propose to do is take illocutionary point, and its corollaries, direction of fit and expressed sincerity conditions, as the basis for constructing a classification. In such a classification, other features – the role of authority, discourse relations, etc. – will fall into their appropriate places.

IV. ALTERNATIVE TAXONOMY

In this section, I shall present a list of what I regard as the basic categories of illocutionary acts. In so doing, I shall discuss briefly how my classification relates to Austin's.

Assertives. The point or purpose of the members of the assertive class is to commit the speaker (in varying degrees) to something's being the case, to the truth of the expressed proposition. All of the members of the assertive class are assessable on the dimension of assessment which includes *true* and *false*. Using Frege's assertion sign to mark the illocutionary point common to all the members of this class, and the symbols introduced above, we may symbolize this class as follows:

$$\vdash \downarrow B(p).$$

The direction of fit is words to the world; the psychological state expressed is Belief (that p). It is important to emphasize that words such as "belief" and "commitment" are here intended to mark dimensions, they are so to speak determinables rather than determinates. Thus, there is a difference between *suggesting* that *p* or *putting it forward as a hypothesis* that *p* on the one hand and *insisting* that *p* or solemnly *swearing* that *p* on the other. The degree of belief and commitment may approach or even reach zero, but it is clear or will become clear, that *hypothesizing that p* and *flatly stating that p* are in the same line of business in a way that neither is like requesting. Once we recognize the existence of *assertives* as a quite separate class, based on the notion of illocutionary point, then the existence of a large number of performative verbs that denote illocutions that seem to be assessable in the True–False dimension and yet are not just "statements" will be easily explicable in terms of the fact that they mark features of illocutionary force which are in addition to illocutionary point. Thus, for example, consider: "boast" and "complain". They both denote assertives with the added feature that they have something to do with the interest of the speaker (condition 6 above). "Conclude" and "deduce" are also assertives with the added feature that they mark certain relations between the assertive illocutionary act and the rest of the discourse or the context of utterance (condition 7 above). This class will contain most of Austin's expositives and many of his verdictives as well for the, by now I hope obvious, reason that they all have the same illocutionary point and differ only in other features of illocutionary force. The simplest test of an assertive is this: can you literally characterize it (inter alia) as true or false. Though I hasten to add that this will give neither necessary nor sufficient conditions, as we shall see when we get to my fifth class.

These points about assertives will, I hope, be clearer when I discuss my second class which, with some reluctance, I will call

Directives. The illocutionary point of these consists in the fact that they are attempts (of varying degrees, and hence, more precisely, they are determinates of the determinable which includes attempting) by the speaker to get the hearer to do something. They may be very modest "attempts" as when I invite you to do it or suggest that you do it, or they may be very fierce attempts as when I insist that you do it. Using the shriek mark for the illocutionary point indicating device for the members of this class generally, we have the following symbolism:

$$! \uparrow W\,(H\,\text{does}\,A)$$

The direction of fit is world-to-words and the sincerity condition is want (or wish or desire). The propositional content is always that the hearer *H* does some future action *A*. Verbs denoting members of this class are *ask, order, command, request, beg, plead, pray, entreat,* and also *invite, permit,* and *advise.* I think also that it is clear that *dare, defy* and *challenge* which Austin lists as behabitives are in this class. Many of Austin's exercitives are also in this class. Questions are a subclass of directives, since they are attempts by *S* to get *H* to answer, i.e. to perform a speech act.

Commissives. Austin's definition of commissives seems to me unexceptionable, and I will simply appropriate it as it stands with the cavil that several of the verbs he lists as commissive verbs do not belong in this class at all, such as "shall", "intend", "favor", and others. Commissives then are those illocutionary acts whose point is to committ the speaker (again in varying degrees) to some future course of action. Using "*C*" for the members of this class generally, we have the following symbolism:

$$C \uparrow I\,(S\,\text{does}\,A)$$

The direction of fit is world-to-word and the sincerity condition is Intention. The propositional content is always that the speaker *S* does some future action *A*. Since the direction of fit is the same for commissives and directives, it would give us a more elegant taxonomy if we could show that they are really members of the same category. I am unable to do this because whereas the point of a promise is to commit the speaker to doing something (and not necessarily to try to get himself to do it) the point of a request is to try to get the hearer to do something (and not necessarily to commit or obligate him to do it). In order to assimilate the two categories, one would have to show that promises are really a species of requests to oneself (this has been suggested to me by Julian Boyd) or alternatively one would have to show that requests placed the hearer under an obligation (this has been suggested to me by William Alston and John Kearns). I have been unable to make either of these analyses work and am left with the inelegant solution of two separate categories with the same direction of fit.

A fourth category I shall call,

Expressives. The illocutionary point of this class is to express the psychological state specified in the sincerity condition about a state of affairs specified in the propositional content. The paradigms of expressive verbs are "thank", "congratulate", "apologize", "condole", "deplore", and "welcome". Notice that in expressives there is no direction of fit. In performing an expressive, the speaker is neither trying to get the world to match the words nor the words to match the world, rather the truth of the expressed proposition is presupposed. Thus, for example, when I apologize for having stepped on your toe, it is not my purpose either to claim that your toe was stepped on nor to get it stepped on. This fact is neatly reflected in the syntax (of English) by the fact that the paradigm expressive verbs in their performative occurrence will not take *that* clauses but require a gerundive nominalization transformation (or some other nominal). One cannot say:

* I apologize that I stepped on your toe;
rather the correct English is,
I apologize for stepping on your toe.

Similarly, one cannot have:

* I congratulate you that you won the race

nor

* I thank you that you paid me the money.

One must have:

I congratulate you on winning the race (congratulations on winning the race)
I thank you for paying me the money (thanks for paying me the money).

These syntactical facts, I suggest, are consequences of the fact that there is no direction of fit in expressives. The truth of the proposition expressed in an expressive is presupposed. The symbolization therefore of this class must proceed as follows:

$$E \varnothing (P) (S/H + \text{property})$$

Where "E" indicates the illocutionary point common to all expressives "$\varnothing$" is the null symbol indicating no direction of fit, P is a variable ranging over the different possible psychological states expressed in the performance of the illocutionary acts in this class, and the propositional content ascribes some property (not necessarily an action) to either S or H. I can congratulate you not only on your winning the race, but also on your good looks. The property specified in the propositional content of an expressive must, however, be related to S or H. I cannot without some very special assumptions congratulate you on Newton's first law of motion.

It would be economical if we could include all illocutionary acts in these four classes, and would lend some further support to the general pattern of analysis adopted in *Speech Acts*, but it seems to me the taxonomy is still not complete. There is still left an important class of cases, where the state of affairs represented in the proposition expressed is realized or brought into existence by the illocutionary force indicating device, cases where one brings a state of affairs into existence by declaring it to exist, cases where, so to speak, "saying makes it so". Examples of these cases are "I resign", "You're fired", "I excommunicate you", "I christen this ship the battleship Missouri", "I appoint you chairman", and "War is hereby declared". These cases were presented as paradigms in the very earliest discussions of performatives, but it seems to me they are still not adequately described in the literature and their relation to other kinds of illocutionary acts is usually misunderstood. Let us call this class,

Declarations. It is the defining characteristic of this class that the successful performance of one of its members brings about the correspondence between the propositional content and reality, successful performance guarantees that the propositional content corresponds to the world: if I successfully perform the act of appointing you chairman, then you are chairman; if I successfully perform the act of nominating you as candidate, then you are a candidate; if I successfully perform the act of declaring a state of war, then war is on; if I successfully perform the act of marrying you, then you are married.

The surface syntactical structure of many sentences used to perform declarations conceals this point from us because in them there is no surface syntactical distinction between propositional content and illocutionary force. Thus, "You're fired" and "I resign" do not seem to permit a distinction between illocutionary force and propositional content, but I think in fact that in their use to perform declarations their semantic structure is:

I declare: your employment is (hereby) terminated
I declare: my position is (hereby) terminated.

Declarations bring about some alteration in the status or condition of the referred to object or objects solely in virtue of the fact that the declaration has been successfully performed. This feature of declarations distinguishes them from the other categories. In the history of the discussion of these topics since Austin's first introduction of his distinction between performatives and constatives, this feature of declarations has not been properly understood. The original distinction between constatives and performatives was supposed to be a distinction between utterances which are sayings (constatives, statements, assertions, etc.) and utterances which are doings (promises, bets, warnings, etc.). What I am calling declarations were included in the class of performatives. The main theme of Austin's mature work, *How to Do Things with Words*, is that this distinction collapses. Just as saying certain things constitutes getting married (a "performative") and saying certain things constitutes making a promise (another "performative"), so saying certain things constitutes making a statement (supposedly a "constative"). As Austin saw but as many philosophers still fail to see, the parallel is exact. Making a statement is as much performing an illocutionary act as making a promise, a bet, a warning or what have you. Any utterance will consist in performing one or more illocutionary acts.

The illocutionary force indicating device in the sentence operates on the propositional content to indicate among other things the direction of fit between the propositional content and reality. In the case of assertives, the direction of fit is words-to-world, in the case of directives and commissives, it is world-to-words; in the case of expressives there is no direction of fit carried by the illocutionary force because the existence of fit is presupposed. The utterance can't get off the ground unless there already is a fit. But now with the declarations we discover a very peculiar relation. The performance of a declaration brings about a fit by its very successful performance. How is such a thing possible?

Notice that all of the examples we have considered so far involve an extra-linguistic institution, a system of constitutive rules in addition to the constitutive rules of language, in order that the declaration may be successfully performed. The mastery of those rules which constitute linguistic competence by the speaker and hearer is not in general sufficient for the performance of a declaration. In addition, there must exist an extra-linguistic institution and the speaker and hearer must occupy special places within this institution. It is only given such institutions as the church, the law, private property, the state and a special position of the speaker and hearer within these institutions that one can excommunicate, appoint, give and bequeath one's possessions or declare war. There are two classes of exceptions to the principle that every declaration requires an extra-linguistic institution. First there are supernatural declarations. When, e.g., God says "Let there be light" that is a declaration. Secondly there are declarations that concern language itself, as for example, when one says, "I define, abbreviate, name, call or dub." Austin sometimes talks as if all performatives (and in the general theory, all illocutionary acts) required an extra-linguistic institution, but this is plainly not the case. Declarations are a very special category of speech acts. We shall symbolize their structure as follows:

$$D \updownarrow \varnothing \, (p)$$

Where D indicates the declarational illocutionary point; the direction of fit is both words-to-world and world-to-words because of the peculiar character of declarations; there is no sincerity condition, hence we have the null symbol in the sincerity condition slot; and we use the usual propositional variable "p".

The reason there has to be a relation of fit arrow here at all is that declarations do attempt to get language to match the world. But they do not attempt to do it either by describing an existing state of affairs (as do assertives) nor by trying to get someone to bring about a future state of affairs (as do directives and commissives).

Some members of the class of declarations overlap with members of the class as assertives. This is because in certain institutional situations we not only ascertain the facts but we need an authority to lay down a decision as to what the facts are after the fact-finding procedure has been gone through. The argument must eventually come to an end and issue in a decision, and it is for this reason that we have judges and umpires. Both, the judge and the umpire, make factual claims; "you are out", "you are guilty". Such claims are clearly assessable in the dimension of word–world fit. Was he really tagged off base? Did he really commit the crime? They are assessable in the word-to-world dimension. But, at the same time, both have the force of declarations. If the umpire calls you out (and is upheld on appeal), then for baseball purposes you are out regardless of the facts in the case, and if the judge declares you guilty (and is upheld on appeal), then for legal purposes you are guilty. There is nothing mysterious about these cases. Institutions characteristically require illocutionary acts to be issued by authorities of various kinds which have the force of declarations. Some institutions require assertive claims to be issued with the force of declarations in order that the argument over the truth of the claim can come to an end somewhere and the next institutional steps which wait on the settling of the factual issue can proceed: the prisoner is released or sent to jail, the side is retired, a touchdown is scored. The existence of this class we may dub "Assertive declarations". Unlike the other declarations, they share with assertives a sincerity condition. The judge, jury and umpire can logically speaking lie, but the man who declares war or nominates you cannot lie in the performance of his illocutionary act. The symbolism for the class of assertive declarations, then, is this:

$$D_a \downarrow\updownarrow B(p)$$

where "D_a" indicates the illocutionary point of issuing an assertive with the force of a declaration, the first arrow indicates the assertive direction of fit, the second indicates the declarational direction of fit, the sincerity condition is belief and the "p" represents the propositional content.

V. SOME SYNTACTICAL ASPECTS OF THE CLASSIFICATION

So far, I have been classifying illocutionary acts, and have used facts about verbs for evidence and illustration. In this section, I want to discuss explicitly some points about English syntax. If the distinctions marked in section IV are of any real significance, they are likely to have various syntactical consequences, and I now propose to examine the deep structure of explicit performative sentences in each of the five categories; that is, I want to examine the syntactical structure of sentences containing the performative occurrence of appropriate illocutionary verbs for each of the five categories. Since all of the sentences we will be considering will contain a performative verb in the main clause, and a subordinate clause, I will abbreviate the usual tree structures in the following fashion: The sentence, e.g., "I predict John will hit Bill", has the deep structure shown in Figure 1. I will simply abbreviate this as: I predict + John will hit Bill. Parentheses will be used to mark optional elements or elements that are obligatory only for a restricted class of the verbs in question. Where there is a choice of one

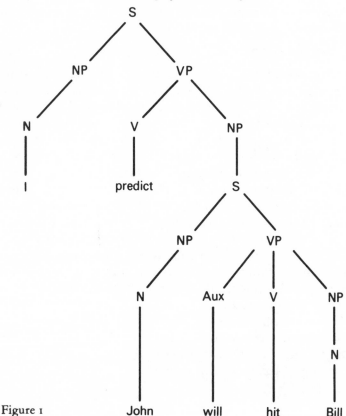

A taxonomy of illocutionary acts

Figure 1

of two elements, I will put a stroke between the elements, e.g. I/you.

Assertives. The deep structure of such paradigm assertive sentences as "I state that it is raining" and "I predict he will come" is simply, I verb (that) + S. This class, as a class, provides no further constraints; though particular verbs may provide further constraints on the lower node S. For example, "predict" requires that an Aux in the lower S must be future or, at any rate, cannot be past. Such assertive verbs as "describe", "call", "classify", and "identify" take a different syntactical structure, similar to many verbs of declaration, and I shall discuss them later.

Directives. Such sentences as "I order you to leave" and "I

21

command you to stand at attention" have the following deep structure:

I verb you + you Fut Vol Verb (NP) (Adv).

"I order you to leave" is thus the surface structure realization of "I order you + you will leave" with equi NP deletion of the repeated "you". Notice that an additional syntactical argument for my including "dare", "defy", and "challenge", in my list of directive verbs and objecting to Austin's including them with "apologize", "thank", "congratulate", etc., is that they have the same syntactical form as do the paradigm directive verbs "order", "command", and "request". Similarly, "invite", and "advise" (in one of its senses) have the directive syntax. "Permit" also has the syntax of directives, though giving permission is not strictly speaking trying to get someone to do something, rather it consists in removing antecedently existing restrictions on his doing it, and is therefore the illocutionary negation of a directive with a negative propositional content, its logical form is $\sim !(\sim p)$.

Commissives. Such sentences as "I promise to pay you the money", and "I pledge allegiance to the flag", and "I vow to get revenge", have the deep structure

I verb (you) + I Fut Vol Verb (NP) (Adv).

Thus, "I promise to pay you the money", is the surface structure realization of "I promise you + I will pay you the money", with equi NP deletion of the repeated "I". We hear the difference in syntax between "I promise you to come on Wednesday" and "I order you to come on Wednesday" as being that "I" is the deep structure subject of "come" in the first and "you" is the deep structure subject of "come" in the second, as required by the verbs "promise" and "order" respectively. Notice that not all of the paradigm commissives have "you" as an indirect object of the performative verb. In the sentence "I pledge allegiance to the flag" the deep structure is not "I pledge to you flag + I will be allegiant." It is

I pledge + I will be allegiant to the flag.

22

Whereas there are purely syntactical arguments that such paradigm directive verbs as "order", and "command", as well as the imperative mood require "you" as the deep structure subject of the lower node S, I do not know of any syntactical argument to show that commissives require "I" as the deep structure subject on their lower node S. Semantically, indeed, we must interpret such sentences as "I promise that Henry will be here on Wednesday" as meaning

I promise that *I will see to it* that Henry will be here next Wednesday,

insofar as we interpret the utterance as a genuine promise, but I know of no purely syntactical arguments to show that the deep structure of the former sentence contains the italicized elements in the latter.

Expressives. As I mentioned earlier, expressives characteristically require a gerundive transformation of the verb in the lower node S. We say:

I apologize for stepping on your toe
I congratulate you on winning the race
I thank you for giving me the money.

The deep structure of such sentences is:

I verb you + I/you VP ⇒ gerundive nom.

And, to repeat, the explanation of the obligatory gerundive is that there is no direction of fit. The forms that standardly admit of questions concerning direction of fit, *that* clauses and infinitives, are impermissible. Hence, the impossibility of

* I congratulate you that you won the race
* I apologize to step on your toe.

However, not all of the permissible nominalization transformations are gerundive; the point is only that they must not produce *that* clauses or infinitive phrases, thus, we can have either

I apologize for behaving badly

or

I apologize for my bad behaviour

but not,

* I apologize that I behaved badly
* I apologize to behave badly.

Before considering declarations, I want now to resume discussion of those assertive verbs which have a different syntax from the paradigms above. I have said that the paradigm assertives have the syntactical form

I verb (that) + S.

But, if we consider such assertive verbs as "diagnose", "call", and "describe", as well as, "class", "classify", and "identify", we find that they do not fit this pattern at all. Consider "call", "describe", and "diagnose", in such sentences as

I call him a liar
I diagnose his case as appendicitis, and
I describe John as a Fascist.

In general the form of this is

I verb NP_1 + NP_1 be pred.

One cannot say

* I call that he is a liar.
* I diagnose that his case is appendicitis (perversely, some of my students find this form acceptable)
* I describe that John is a Fascist.

There, therefore, seems to be a very severe set of restrictions on an important class of assertive verbs which is not shared by the other paradigms. Would this justify us in concluding that these verbs were wrongly classed as assertives along with "state", "assert", "claim" and "predict" and that we need a separate class for them? It might be argued that the existence of these verbs substantiates Austin's claim that we require a separate class of verdictives distinct from expositives, but that would surely be a very curious conclusion to draw since Austin lists most of the verbs we mentioned above as expositives. He includes "describe", "class", "identify" and "call" as expositives and "diagnose" and "describe" as verdictives. A common syntax of many verdictives and expositives would hardly warrant the need for verdictives as a separate class. But leaving aside Austin's taxonomy, the question still arises, do we require a separate semantic category to account for these syntactical facts? I think not. I think there is a much simpler explanation of the distribution of these verbs. Often, in assertive discourse, we focus our attention on some topic of discussion. The question is not just what is the propositional content we are asserting, but what do we say about the *object*(s) referred to in the propositional content: not just what do we state, claim, characterize, or assert, but how do we describe, call, diagnose or identify *it*, some previously referred to topic of discussion. When, for example, there is a question of diagnosing or describing it is always a question of diagnosing a person or his case, of describing a landscape or a party or a person, etc. These assertive illocutionary verbs give us a device for isolating topics from what is said about topics. But this very genuine syntactical difference does not mark a semantic difference big enough to justify the formation of a separate category. Notice in support of my argument here that the actual sentences in which the describing, diagnosing, etc., is done are seldom of the explicit performative type, but rather are usually in the standard indicative forms which are so characteristic of the assertive class.

Utterances of:

He is a liar
He has appendicitis
He is a Fascist

are all characteristically *statements*, in the making of which we call, diagnose, and describe, as well as, accuse, identify, and characterize. I conclude then that there are typically two syntactical forms for assertive illocutionary verbs; one of which focusses on propositional content, the other on the object(s) referred to in the propositional content, but both of which are semantically assertives.

Declarations. I mention the syntactical form

I verb $NP_1 + NP_1$ be pred

both to forestall an argument for erecting a separate semantic category for them and because many verbs of declaration have this form. Indeed, there appear to be several different syntactical forms for explicit performatives of declaration. I believe the following three classes are the most important.

1. I find you guilty as charged
   I now pronounce you man and wife
   I appoint you chairman
2. War is hereby declared
   I declare the meeting adjourned
3. You're fired
   I resign
   I excommunicate you.

The deep syntactical structure of these three, respectively, is as follows:

1. I verb $NP_1 + NP_1$ be pred.

Thus, in our examples, we have

I find you + you be guilty as charged
I pronounce you + you be man and wife
I appoint you + you be chairman
2. I declare + S.

Thus, in our examples we have

I/we (hereby) declare + a state of war exists
I declare + the meeting be adjourned.

This form is the purest form of the declaration: the speaker in authority brings about a state of affairs specified in the propositional content by saying in effect, I declare the state of affairs to exist. Semantically, all declarations are of this character, though in class 1 the focussing on the topic produces an alteration in the syntax which is exactly the same syntax as we saw in such assertive verbs as "describe", "characterize", "call", and "diagnose" and in class 3 the syntax conceals the semantic structure even more.

3. The syntax of these is the most misleading. It is simply
   I verb (NP)

as in our examples,

I fire you
I resign
I excommunicate you.

The semantic structure of these, however, seems to me the same as class 2. "You're fired," if uttered as performance of the act of firing someone and not as a report means

I declare + your job is terminated.

Similarly, "I hereby resign" means

I hereby declare + my job is terminated.

"I excommunicate you" means

I declare + your membership in the church is terminated.

The explanation for the bemusingly simple syntactical structure of these sentences seems to me to be that we have some verbs which in their performative occurrence encapsulate both the declarative force and the propositional content.

VI. CONCLUSIONS

We are now in a position to draw certain general conclusions.
   1. Many of the verbs we call illocutionary verbs are not markers of illocutionary point but of some other feature of the illocutionary act. Consider "insist" and "suggest". I can insist that we go to the movies or I can suggest that we go to the movies; but I can also insist that the answer is found on p. 16 or I can suggest that it is found on p. 16. The first pair are directives, the second, assertives. Does this show that insisting and suggesting are different illocutionary acts altogether from assertives and directives, or perhaps that they are both assertives and directives? I think the answer to both

questions is no. Both "insist" and "suggest" are used to mark the degree of intensity with which the illocutionary point is presented. They do not mark a separate illocutionary point at all. Similarly, "announce", "hint", and "confide", do not mark separate illocutionary points but rather the style or manner of performance of an illocutionary act. Paradoxical as it may sound, such verbs are illocutionary verbs, but not names of kinds of illocutionary acts. It is for this reason, among others, that we must carefully distinguish a taxonomy of illocutionary acts from one of illocutionary verbs.

2. In section IV, I tried to classify illocutionary acts and, in section V, I tried to explore some of the syntactical features of the verbs denoting member of each of the categories. But, I have not attempted to classify illocutionary verbs. If one did so, I believe the following would emerge.

(a) First, as just noted, some verbs do not mark illocutionary point at all, but some other feature, e.g. "insist", "suggest", "announce", "confide", "reply", "answer", "interject", "remark", "ejaculate" and "interpose".

(b) Many verbs mark illocutionary point plus some other feature, e.g. "boast", "lament", "threaten", "criticize", "accuse", and "warn" all add the feature of goodness or badness to their primary illocutionary point.

(c) Some few verbs mark more than one illocutionary point, e.g. a *protest* involves both an expression of disapproval and a petition for change.

Promulgating a law has both a declarational status (the propositional content becomes law) and a directive status (the law is directive in intent). The verbs of assertive declaration fall into this class.

(d) Some few verbs can take more than one illocutionary point. Consider "warn" and "advise". Notice that both of these take either the directive syntax or the assertive syntax. Thus,

I warn you to stay away from my wife!	(directive)
I warn you that the bull is about to charge	(assertive)
I advise you to leave	(directive)

Passengers are hereby advised that the train
will be late   (assertive).
Correspondingly, it seems to me, that warning and advising
may be either telling you *that* something is the case (with
relevance to what is or is not in your interest) or telling you *to*
do something about it (because it is or is not in your interest).
They can be, but need not be, both at once.

3. The most important conclusion to be drawn from this
discussion in this. There are not, as Wittgenstein (on one
possible interpretation)˙ and many others have claimed, an
infinite or indefinite number of language games or uses of
language. Rather, the illusion of limitless uses of language is
engendered by an enormous unclarity about what constitutes
the criteria for delimiting one language game or use of
language from another. If we adopt illocutionary point as the
basic notion on which to classify uses of language, then there
are a rather limited number of basic things we do with
language: we tell people how things are, we try to get them to
do things, we commit ourselves to doing things, we express
our feelings and attitudes and we bring about changes
through our utterances. Often, we do more than one of these
at once in the same utterance.

Chapter 2

INDIRECT SPEECH ACTS

INTRODUCTION

The simplest cases of meaning are those in which the speaker utters a sentence and means exactly and literally what he says. In such cases the speaker intends to produce a certain illocutionary effect in the hearer, and he intends to produce this effect by getting the hearer to recognize his intention to produce it, and he intends to get the hearer to recognize this intention in virtue of the hearer's knowledge of the rules that govern the utterance of the sentence. But, notoriously, not all cases of meaning are this simple: In hints, insinuations, irony, and metaphor – to mention a few examples – the speaker's utterance meaning and the sentence meaning come apart in various ways. One important class of such cases is that in which the speaker utters a sentence, means what he says, but also means something more. For example, a speaker may utter the sentence "I want you to do it" by way of requesting the hearer to do something. The utterance is incidentally meant as a statement, but it is also meant primarily as a request, a request made by way of making a statement. In such cases a sentence that contains the illocutionary force indicators for one kind of illocutionary act can be uttered to perform, *in addition*, another type of illocutionary act. There are also cases in which the speaker may utter a sentence and mean what he says and also mean another illocution with a different propositional content. For example, a speaker may utter the sentence "Can you reach the salt?" and mean it not merely as a question but as a request to pass the salt.

In such cases it is important to emphasize that the utterance is meant as a request; that is, the speaker intends to produce in the hearer the knowledge that a request has been made to him, and he intends to produce this knowledge by means of getting the hearer to recognize his intention to produce it. Such cases, in which the utterance has two illocutionary forces, are to be sharply distinguished from the cases in which, for example, the speaker tells the hearer that he wants him to do something; and then the hearer does it because the speaker wants him to, though no request at all has been made, meant, or understood. The cases we will be discussing are indirect speech acts, cases in which one illocutionary act is performed indirectly by way of performing another.

The problem posed by indirect speech acts is the problem of how it is possible for the speaker to say one thing and mean that but also to mean something else. And since meaning consists in part in the intention to produce understanding in the hearer, a large part of that problem is that of how it is possible for the hearer to understand the indirect speech act when the sentence he hears and understands means something else. The problem is made more complicated by the fact that some sentences seem almost to be conventionally used as indirect requests. For a sentence like "Can you reach the salt?" or "I would appreciate it if you would get off my foot", it takes some ingenuity to imagine a situation in which their utterances would not be requests.

In Searle (1969: chapter 3) I suggested that many such utterances could be explained by the fact that the sentences in question concern conditions of the felicitous performance of the speech acts they are used to perform indirectly – preparatory conditions, propositional content conditions, and sincerity conditions – and that their use to perform indirect speech acts consists in indicating the satisfaction of an essential condition by means of asserting or questioning one of the other conditions. Since that time a variety of explanations have been proposed, involving such things as the hypostatization of "conversational postulates" or alternative deep structures. The answer originally suggested in Searle (1969) seems to me incomplete, and I want to develop it further here. The hypothesis I wish to defend is simply this: In indirect speech acts the speaker communicates to the hearer more than he actually says by way of relying on their mutually shared background information, both linguistic and nonlinguistic, together with the general powers of rationality and inference on the part of the hearer. To be more specific, the apparatus necessary to explain the indirect part of indirect speech acts includes a theory of speech acts, certain general principles of cooperative conversation (some of which have been discussed by Grice (1975)), and mutually shared factual background information of the speaker and the hearer, together with an ability on the part of the hearer to make inferences. It is not necessary to assume the existence of any conversational postulates (either as an addition to the theory of speech acts or as part of the theory of speech acts) nor any concealed imperative forces or other ambiguities. We will see, however, that in some cases, convention plays a most peculiar role.

Aside from its interest for a theory of meaning and speech acts, the problem of indirect speech acts is of philosophical importance for an additional reason. In ethics it has commonly been supposed that "good", "right", "ought", etc. somehow have an imperative or "action guiding" meaning. This view derives from the fact that sentences such as "You ought to do it" are often uttered by way of telling the hearer to do something. But from the fact that such sentences can be uttered as directives[1] it no more follows that "ought" has an imperative meaning than from the fact that "Can you reach the salt?" can be uttered as a request to pass the salt it follows that *can* has an imperative meaning. Many confusions in recent moral philosophy rest on a failure to understand the nature of such indirect speech acts. The topic has an additional interest for linguists because of its syntactical consequences, but I shall be concerned with these only incidentally.

---

[1] The class of "directive" illocutionary acts includes acts of ordering, commanding, requesting, pleading, begging, praying, entreating, instructing, forbidding, and others. See Searle (1975a, chapter 1 of this volume) for an explanation of this notion.

Indirect speech acts

Let us begin by considering a typical case of the general phenomenon of indirection:

1. Student X: Let's go to the movies tonight
2. Student Y: I have to study for an exam.

The utterance of (1) constitutes a proposal in virtue of its meaning, in particular because of the meaning of "Let's". In general, literal utterances of sentences of this form will constitute proposals, as in:

3. Let's eat pizza tonight

or:

4. Let's go ice skating tonight.

The utterance of 2 in the context just given would normally constitute a rejection of the proposal, but not in virtue of its meaning. In virtue of its meaning it is simply a statement about Y. Statements of this form do not, in general, constitute rejections of proposals, even in cases in which they are made in response to a proposal. Thus, if Y had said:

5. I have to eat popcorn tonight

or:

6. I have to tie my shoes

in a normal context, neither of these utterances would have been a rejection of the proposal. The question then arises, How does X know that the utterance is a rejection of the proposal? and that question is a part of the question, How is it possible for Y to intend or mean the utterance of 2 as a rejection of the proposal? In order to describe this case, let us introduce some terminology. Let us say that the *primary* illocutionary act performed in Y's utterance is the rejection of the proposal made by X, and that Y does that by way of performing a *secondary* illocutionary act of making a statement to the effect that he has to prepare for an exam. He performs the secondary illocutionary act by way of uttering a sentence the *literal* meaning of which is such that its literal utterance

33

constitutes a performance of that illocutionary act. We may, therefore, further say that the secondary illocutionary act is literal; the primary illocutionary act is not literal. Let us assume that we know how X understands the literal secondary illocutionary act from the utterance of the sentence. The question is, How does he understand the nonliteral primary illocutionary act from understanding the literal secondary illocutionary act? And that question is part of the larger question, How is it possible for Y to mean the primary illocution when he only utters a sentence that means the secondary illocution, since to mean the primary illocution is (in large part) to intend to produce in X the relevant understanding?

A brief reconstruction of the steps necessary to derive the primary illocution from the literal illocution would go as follows. (In normal conversation, of course, no one would consciously go through the steps involved in this reasoning.)

Step 1: I have made a proposal to Y, and in response he has made a statement to the effect that he has to study for an exam (facts about the conversation).

Step 2: I assume that Y is cooperating in the conversation and that therefore his remark is intended to be relevant (principles of conversational cooperation).

Step 3: A relevant response must be one of acceptance, rejection, counterproposal, further discussion, etc. (theory of speech acts).

Step 4: But his literal utterance was not one of these, and so was not a relevant response (inference from Steps 1 and 3).

Step 5: Therefore, he probably means more than he says. Assuming that his remark is relevant, his primary illocutionary point must differ from his literal one (inference from Steps 2 and 4).[2]

This step is crucial. Unless a hearer has some inferential strategy for finding out when primary illocutionary points differ from literal illocutionary points, he has no way of understanding indirect illocutionary acts.

---

[2] For an explanation of the notion of "illocutionary point" and its relation to illocutionary force, see (Searle, 1975a, chapter 1 of this volume).

Step 6: I know that studying for an exam normally takes a large amount of time relative to a single evening, and I know that going to the movies normally takes a large amount of time relative to a single evening (factual background information).

Step 7: Therefore, he probably cannot both go to the movies and study for an exam in one evening (inference from Step 6).

Step 8: A preparatory condition on the acceptance of a proposal, or on any other commissive, is the ability to perform the act predicated in the propositional content condition (theory of speech acts).

Step 9: Therefore, I know that he has said something that has the consequence that he probably cannot consistently accept the proposal (inference from Steps 1, 7, and 8).

Step 10: Therefore, his primary illocutionary point is probably to reject the proposal (inference from Steps 5 and 9).

It may seem somewhat pedantic to set all of this out in 10 steps; but if anything, the example is still underdescribed – I have not, for example, discussed the role of the assumption of sincerity, or the ceteris paribus conditions that attach to various of the steps. Notice, also, that the conclusion is probabilistic. It is and ought to be. This is because the reply does not necessarily constitute a rejection of the proposal. *Y* might have gone on to say:

7. I have to study for an exam, but let's go to the movies anyhow

or:

8. I have to study for an exam, but I'll do it when we get home from the movies.

The inferential strategy is to establish, first, that the primary illocutionary point departs from the literal, and second, what the primary illocutionary point is.

The argument of this chapter will be that the theoretical apparatus used to explain this case will suffice to explain the general phenomenon of indirect illocutionary acts. That apparatus includes mutual background information, a theory of speech acts, and certain general principles of conversation. In particular, we explained this case without having to assume that sentence 2 is ambiguous or that it is "ambiguous in context" or that it is necessary to assume the existence of any "conversational postulates" in order to explain *X*'s understanding the primary illocution of the utterance. The main difference between this case and the cases we will be discussing is that the latter all have a generality of *form* that is lacking in this example. I shall mark this generality by using bold type for the formal features in the surface structure of the sentences in question. In the field of indirect illocutionary acts, the area of directives is the most useful to study because ordinary conversational requirements of politeness normally make it awkward to issue flat imperative sentences (e.g. "Leave the room") or explicit performatives (e.g. "I order you to leave the room"), and we therefore seek to find indirect means to our illocutionary ends (e.g. "I wonder if you would mind leaving the room"). In directives, politeness is the chief motivation for indirectness.

SOME SENTENCES "CONVENTIONALLY" USED IN THE PERFORMANCE OF INDIRECT DIRECTIVES

Let us begin, then, with a short list of some of the sentences that could quite standardly be used to make indirect requests and other directives such as orders. At a pretheoretical level these sentences naturally tend to group themselves into certain categories.[3]

Group 1 : Sentences concerning H's ability to perform A :
Can you reach the salt?
Can you pass the salt?
Could you be a little more quiet?
You could be a little more quiet
You can go now (*this may also be a permission* = you may go now)

---

[3] In what follows, I use the letters *H*, *S*, and *A* as abbreviations for "hearer", "speaker", and "act" or "action".

Are you able to reach the book on the
   top shelf?
Have you got change for a dollar?

Group 2: Sentences concerning S's wish or want that H will do A :

I would like you to go now
I want you to do this for me, Henry
I would/should appreciate it if you
   would/could do it for me
I would/should be most grateful if
   you would/could help us out
I'd rather you didn't do that any more
I'd be very much obliged if you would
   pay me the money back soon
I hope you'll do it
I wish you wouldn't do that.

Group 3: Sentences concerning H's doing A :

Officers **will** henceforth wear ties at
   dinner
Will you quit making that awful racket?
Would you kindly get off my foot?
Won't you stop making that noise soon?
Aren't you going to eat your cereal?

Group 4: Sentences concerning H's desire or willingness to do A :

Would you be willing to write a letter
   of recommendation for me?
Do you want to hand me that hammer over
   there on the table?
Would you mind not making so much noise?
Would it be convenient for you to come
   on Wednesday?
Would it be too much (trouble) for you
   to pay me the money next Wednesday?

Group 5: Sentences concerning reasons for doing A :

You ought to be more polite to your mother

You should leave immediately
Must you continue hammering that way?
Ought you to eat quite so much spaghetti?
Should you be wearing John's tie?
You had better go now
Hadn't you better go now?
Why not stop here?
Why don't you try it just once?
Why don't you be quiet?
It would be better for you (for us all)
    if you would leave the room
It wouldn't hurt if you left now
It might help if you shut up
It would be better if you gave me the
    money now
It would be a good idea if you left town
We'd all be better off if you'd just
    pipe down a bit.

This class also contains many examples that have no generality of form but obviously, in an appropriate context, would be uttered as indirect requests, e.g.:

You're standing on my foot
I can't see the movie screen while
    you have that hat on.

Also in this class belong, possibly:

How many times have I told you (must I
    tell you) not to eat with your fingers?
I must have told you a dozen times not
    to eat with your mouth open
If I have told you once I have told you
    a thousand times not to wear your hat in
    the house.

Group 6: Sentences embedding one of these elements inside another; also, sentences embedding an explicit directive illocutionary verb inside one of these contexts.

Would you mind awfully if I asked you

if you could write me a letter of
recommendation?
**Would it be too much if I suggested
that you could possibly** make a little
less noise?
Might I ask you to take off your hat?
**I hope you won't mind if I ask you if
you could** leave us alone
I would appreciate it if you could
make less noise.[4]

This is a very large class, since most of its members are
constructed by permuting certain of the elements of the other
classes.

SOME PUTATIVE FACTS

Let us begin by noting several salient facts about the
sentences in question. Not everyone will agree that what
follows are facts; indeed, most of the available explanations
consist in denying one or more of these statements.
Nonetheless, at an intuitive pretheoretical level each of the
following would seem to be correct observations about the
sentences in question, and I believe we should surrender
these intuitions only in the face of very serious counterargu-
ments. I will eventually argue that an explanation can be
given that is consistent with all of these facts.

*Fact 1 : The sentences in question do not have an imperative force as
part of their meaning.* This point is sometimes denied by
philosophers and linguists, but very powerful evidence
for it is provided by the fact that it is possible without
inconsistency to connect the literal utterance of one of these
forms with the denial of any imperative intent, e.g.:

I'd like you to do this for me, Bill, but I am not asking you to
do it or requesting that you do it or ordering you to do it or
telling you to do it

---

[4] This form is also included in Group 2.

I'm just asking you, Bill: Why not eat beans? But in asking you that I want you to understand that I am not telling you to eat beans; I just want to know your reasons for thinking you ought not to.

Fact 2: The sentences in question are not ambiguous as between an imperative illocutionary force and a nonimperative illocutionary force. I think this is intuitively apparent, but in any case, an ordinary application of Occam's razor places the onus of proof on those who wish to claim that these sentences are ambiguous. One does not multiply meanings beyond necessity. Notice, also, that it is no help to say they are "ambiguous in context", for all that means is that one cannot always tell from what the sentence means what the speaker means by its utterance, and that is not sufficient to establish sentential ambiguity.

Fact 3: Notwithstanding Facts 1 and 2, these are standardly, ordinarily, normally – indeed, I shall argue, conventionally – used to issue directives. There is a systematic relation between these and directive illocutions in a way that there is no systematic relation between "I have to study for an exam" and rejecting proposals. Additional evidence that they are standardly used to issue imperatives is that most of them take "please", either at the end of the sentence or preceding the verb, e.g.:

I want you to stop making that noise, please
Could you please lend me a dollar?

When "please" is added to one of these sentences, it explicitly and literally marks the primary illocutionary point of the utterance as directive, even though the literal meaning of the rest of the sentence is not directive.

It is because of the combination of Facts 1, 2, and 3 that there is a problem about these cases at all.

Fact 4: The sentences in question are not, in the ordinary sense, idioms.[5] An ordinary example of an idiom is "kicked the

---

[5] There are some idioms in this line of business, however, for example, "How about" as used in proposals and requests: "How about going to the movies tonight?" "How about giving me some more beer?"

bucket" in "Jones kicked the bucket." The most powerful evidence I know that these sentences are not idioms is that in their use as indirect directives they admit of literal responses that presuppose that they are uttered literally. Thus, an utterance of "Why don't you be quiet, Henry?" admits as a response an utterance of "Well, Sally, there are several reasons for not being quiet. First, . . ." Possible exceptions to this are occurrences of "would" and "could" in indirect speech acts, and I will discuss them later.

Further evidence that they are not idioms is that, whereas a word-for-word translation of "Jones kicked the bucket" into other languages will not produce a sentence meaning "Jones died", translations of the sentences in question will often, though by no means always, produce sentences with the same indirect illocutionary act potential of the English examples. Thus, e.g., "Pourriez-vous m'aider?" and "Können Sie mir helfen?" can be uttered as indirect requests in French or German. I will later discuss the problem of why some translate with equivalent indirect illocutionary force potential and some do not.

Fact 5: To say they are not idioms is not to say they are not idiomatic. All the examples given are idiomatic in current English, and – what is more puzzling – they are idiomatically used as requests. In general, nonidiomatic equivalents or synonyms would not have the same indirect illocutionary act potential. Thus, "Do you want to hand me the hammer over there on the table?" can be uttered as a request, but "Is it the case that you at present desire to hand me that hammer over there on the table?" has a formal and stilted character that in almost all contexts would eliminate it as a candidate for an indirect request. Furthermore, "Are you able to hand me that hammer?", though idiomatic, does not have the same indirect request potential as "Can you hand me that hammer?" That these sentences are *idiomatic* and are *idiomatically used as directives* is crucial to their role in indirect speech acts. I will say more about the relations of these facts later.

Fact 6: The sentences in question have literal utterances in which they are not also indirect requests. Thus, "Can you reach the salt?" can be uttered as a simple question about your abilities (say, by an orthopedist wishing to know the medical progress of your arm injury). "I want you to leave" can be uttered simply as a statement about one's wants, without any directive intent. At first sight, some of our examples might not appear to satisfy this condition, e.g.:

Why not stop here?
Why don't you be quiet?

But with a little imagination it is easy to construct situations in which utterances of these would be not directives but straightforward questions. Suppose someone had said "We ought not to stop here." Then "Why not stop here?" would be an appropriate question, without necessarily being also a suggestion. Similarly, if someone had just said "I certainly hate making all this racket", an utterance of "(Well, then) Why don't you be quiet?" would be an appropriate response, without also necessarily being a request to be quiet.

It is important to note that the intonation of these sentences when they are uttered as indirect requests often differs from their intonation when uttered with only their literal illocutionary force, and often the intonation pattern will be that characteristic of literal directives.

Fact 7: In cases where these sentences are uttered as requests, they still have their literal meaning and are uttered with and as having that literal meaning. I have seen it claimed that they have different meanings "in context" when they are uttered as requests, but I believe that is obviously false. The man who says "I want you to do it" means literally that he wants you to do it. The point is that, as is always the case with indirection, he means not only what he says but something more as well. What is added in the indirect cases is not any additional or different *sentence* meaning, but additional *speaker* meaning. Evidence that these sentences keep their literal meanings when uttered as indirect requests is that responses that are appropriate to their literal utterances are appropriate to their indirect speech act utterances (as we noted in our discussion of Fact 4), e.g.:

Can you pass the salt?
No, sorry, I can't, it's down there at the end of the table
Yes, I can. (Here it is).

Fact 8 : It is a consequence of Fact 7 that when one of these sentences is uttered with the primary illocutionary point of a directive, the literal illocutionary act is also performed. In every one of these cases, the speaker issues a directive *by way of* asking a question or making a statement. But the fact that his primary illocutionary intent is directive does not alter the fact that he is asking a question or making a statement. Additional evidence for Fact 8 is that a subsequent report of the utterances can truly report the literal illocutionary act.

Thus, e.g., the utterance of "I want you to leave now, Bill" can be reported by an utterance of "He told me he wanted me to leave, so I left." Or, the utterance of "Can you reach the salt?" can be reported by an utterance of "He asked me whether I could reach the salt." Similarly, an utterance of "Could you do it for me, Henry; could you do it for me and Cynthia and the children?" can be reported by an utterance of "He asked me whether I could do it for him and Cynthia and the children."

This point is sometimes denied. I have seen it claimed that the literal illocutionary acts are always defective or are not "conveyed" when the sentence is used to perform a nonliteral primary illocutionary act. As far as our examples are concerned, the literal illocutions are always conveyed and are sometimes, but not in general, defective. For example, an indirect speech act utterance of "Can you reach the salt?" may be defective in the sense that S may already know the answer. But even this form *need* not be defective. (Consider, e.g., "Can you give me change for a dollar?") Even when the literal utterance is defective, the indirect speech act does not depend on its being defective.

AN EXPLANATION IN TERMS OF THE THEORY OF SPEECH ACTS

The difference between the example concerning the proposal

to go to the movies and all of the other cases is that the other cases are systematic. What we need to do, then, is to describe an example in such a way as to show how the apparatus used on the first example will suffice for these other cases and also will explain the systematic character of the other cases.

I think the theory of speech acts will enable us to provide a simple explanation of how these sentences, which have one illocutionary force as part of their meaning, can be used to perform an act with a different illocutionary force. Each type of illocutionary act has a set of conditions that are necessary for the successful and felicitous performance of the act. To illustrate this, I will present the conditions on two types of acts within the two genuses, directive and commissive (Searle, 1969: chapter 3).

A comparison of the list of felicity conditions on the directive class of illocutionary acts and our list of types of sentences used to perform indirect directives shows that Groups 1–6 of types can be reduced to three types: those having to do with felicity conditions on the performance of a directive illocutionary act, those having to do with reasons for doing the act, and those embedding one element inside another one. Thus, since the ability of H to perform A (Group 1) is a preparatory condition, the desire of S that H perform A (Group 2) is the sincerity condition, and the predication of A of H (Group 3) is the propositional content condition, all of Groups 1–3 concern felicity conditions on

	Directive (Request)	Commissive (Promise)
Preparatory condition	H is able to perform A.	S is able to perform A. H wants S to perform A.
Sincerity condition	S wants H to do A.	S intends to do A.
Propositional content condition	S predicates a future act A of H.	S predicates a future act A of S.
Essential condition	Counts as an attempt by S to get H to do A.	Counts as the undertaking by S of an obligation to do A.

directive illocutionary acts. Since wanting to do something is a reason par excellence for doing it, Group 4 assimilates to Group 5, as both concern reasons for doing A. Group 6 is a special class only by courtesy, since its elements either are performative verbs or are already contained in the other two categories of felicity conditions and reasons.

Ignoring the embedding cases for the moment, if we look at our lists and our sets of conditions, the following generalizations naturally emerge:

Generalization 1 : S can make an indirect request (or other directive) by either asking whether or stating that a preparatory condition concerning H's ability to do A obtains.

Generalization 2 : S can make an indirect directive by either asking whether or stating that the propositional content condition obtains.

Generalization 3 : S can make an indirect directive by stating that the sincerity condition obtains, but not by asking whether it obtains.

Generalization 4 : S can make an indirect directive by either stating that or asking whether there are good or overriding reasons for doing A, except where the reason is that H wants or wishes, etc., to do A, in which case he can only ask whether H wants, wishes, etc., to do A.

It is the existence of these generalizations that accounts for the systematic character of the relation between the sentences in Groups 1–6 and the directive class of illocutionary acts. Notice that these are generalizations and not rules. The rules of speech acts (or some of them) are stated in the list of conditions presented earlier. That is, for example, it is a rule of the directive class of speech acts that the directive is defective if the hearer is unable to perform the act, but it is precisely not a rule of speech acts or of conversation that one can perform a directive by asking whether the preparatory condition obtains. The theoretical task is to show how that generalization will be a consequence of the rule, together with certain other information, namely, the factual background information and the general principles of conversation.

Our next task is to try to describe an example of an indirect request with at least the same degree of pedantry we used in our description of the rejection of a proposal. Let us take the simplest sort of case: At the dinner table, X says to Y, "Can you pass the salt?" by way of asking Y to pass the salt. Now, how does Y know that X is requesting him to pass the salt instead of just asking a question about his abilities to pass the salt? Notice that not everything will do as a request to pass the salt. Thus, if X had said "Salt is made of sodium chloride" or "Salt is mined in the Tatra mountains", without some special stage setting, it is very unlikely that Y would take either of these utterances as a request to pass the salt. Notice further that, in a normal conversational situation, Y does not have to go through any conscious process of inference to derive the conclusion that the utterance of "Can you pass the salt?" is a request to pass the salt. He simply hears it as a request. This fact is perhaps one of the main reasons why it is tempting to adopt the false conclusion that somehow these examples must have an imperative force as part of their meaning or that they are "ambiguous in context", or some such. What we need to do is offer an explanation that is consistent with all of Facts 1–8 yet does not make the mistake of hypostatizing concealed imperative forces or conversational postulates. A bare-bones reconstruction of the steps necessary for Y to derive the conclusion from the utterance might go roughly as follows:

Step 1: Y has asked me a question as to whether I have the ability to pass the salt (fact about the conversation).

Step 2: I assume that he is cooperating in the conversation and that therefore his utterance has some aim or point (principles of conversational cooperation).

Step 3: The conversational setting is not such as to indicate a theoretical interest in my salt-passing ability (factual background information).

Step 4: Furthermore, he probably already knows that the answer to the question is yes (factual background information). (This step facilitates the move to Step 5, but is not essential).

Step 5: Therefore, his utterance is probably not just a question. It probably has some ulterior illocutionary point (inference from Steps 1, 2, 3, and 4). What can it be?

Step 6: A preparatory condition for any directive illocutionary act

46

is the ability of H to perform the act predicated in the propositional content condition (theory of speech acts).

Step 7: Therefore, X has asked me a question the affirmative answer to which would entail that the preparatory condition for requesting me to pass the salt is satisfied (inference from Steps 1 and 6).

Step 8: We are now at dinner and people normally use salt at dinner; they pass it back and forth, try to get others to pass it back and forth, etc. (background information).

Step 9: He has therefore alluded to the satisfaction of a preparatory condition for a request whose obedience conditions it is quite likely he wants me to bring about (inference from Steps 7 and 8).

Step 10: Therefore, in the absence of any other plausible illocutionary point, he is probably requesting me to pass him the salt (inference from Steps 5 and 9).

The hypothesis being put forth in this chapter is that all the cases can be similarly analyzed. According to this analysis, the reason I can ask you to pass the salt by saying "Can you pass the salt?" but not by saying "Salt is made of sodium chloride" or "Salt is mined in the Tatra mountains" is that your ability to pass the salt is a preparatory condition for requesting you to pass the salt in a way that the other sentences are not related to requesting you to pass the salt. But obviously, that answer is not by itself sufficient, because not all questions about your abilities are requests. The hearer therefore needs some way of finding out when the utterance is just a question about his abilities and when it is a request made by way of asking a question about his abilities. It is at this point that the general principles of conversation (together with factual background information) come into play.

The two features that are crucial, or so I am suggesting, are, first, a strategy for establishing the existence of an ulterior illocutionary point beyond the illocutionary point contained in the meaning of the sentence, and second, a device for finding out what the ulterior illocutionary point is. The first is established by the principles of conversation operating on the information of the hearer and the speaker, and the second is derived from the theory of speech acts together with background information. The generalizations are to be explained by the fact that each of them records a strategy by means of which the hearer can find out how a primary illocutionary point differs from a secondary illocutionary point.

The chief motivation – though not the only motivation – for using these indirect forms is politeness. Notice that, in the example just given, the "Can you" form is polite in at least two respects. Firstly, X does not presume to know about Y's abilities, as he would if he issued an imperative sentence; and, secondly, the form gives – or at least appears to give – Y the option of refusing, since a yes–no question allows *no* as a possible answer. Hence, compliance can be made to appear a free act rather than obeying a command.[6]

SOME PROBLEMS

It is important to emphasize that I have by no means demonstrated the thesis being argued for in this chapter. I have so far only suggested a pattern of analysis that is consistent with the facts. Even supposing that this pattern of analysis could be shown to be successful in many more cases, there are still several problems that remain:

Problem 1: The biggest single problem with the foregoing analysis is this: If, as I have been arguing, the mechanisms by which indirect speech acts are meant and understood are perfectly general – having to do with the theory of speech acts, the principles of cooperative conversation, and shared background information – and not tied to any particular syntactical form, then why is it that some syntactical forms work better than others? Why can I ask you to do something by saying "Can you hand me that book on the top shelf?" but not, or not very easily, by saying "Is it the case that you at present have the ability to hand me that book on the top shelf?"

---

[6] I am indebted to Dorothea Franck for discussion of this point.

Even within such pairs as:

Do you want to do A?
Do you desire to do A?

and:

Can you do A?
Are you able to do A?

there is clearly a difference in indirect illocutionary act potential. Note, for example, that the first member of each pair takes "please" more readily than the second. Granting that none of these pairs are exact synonyms, and granting that all the sentences have some use as indirect requests, it is still essential to explain the differences in their indirect illocutionary act potential. How, in short, can it be the case that some sentences are not imperative idioms and yet function as forms of idiomatic requests?

The first part of the answer is this: The theory of speech acts and the principles of conversational cooperation do, indeed, provide a framework within which indirect illocutionary acts can be meant and understood. However, within this framework certain forms will tend to become conventionally established as the standard idiomatic forms for indirect speech acts. While keeping their literal meanings, they will acquire conventional uses as, e.g., polite forms for requests.

It is by now, I hope, uncontroversial that there is a distinction to be made between meaning and use, but what is less generally recognized is that there can be conventions of usage that are not meaning conventions. I am suggesting that "can you", "could you", "I want you to", and numerous other forms are conventional ways of making requests (and in that sense it is not incorrect to say they are idioms), but at the same time they do not have an imperative meaning (and in that sense it would be incorrect to say they are idioms). Politeness is the most prominent motivation for indirectness in requests, and certain forms naturally tend to become the conventionally polite ways of making indirect requests.

If this explanation is correct, it would go some way toward

explaining why there are differences in the indirect speech forms from one language to another. The mechanisms are not peculiar to this language or that, but at the same time the standard forms from one language will not always maintain their indirect speech act potential when translated from one language to another. Thus, "Can you hand me that book?" will function as an indirect request in English, but its Czech translation, "Můžete mi podat tu Knížku?" will sound very odd if uttered as a request in Czech.

A second part of the answer is this: In order to be a plausible candidate for an utterance as an indirect speech act, a sentence has to be idiomatic to start with. It is very easy to imagine circumstances in which: "Are you able to reach that book on the top shelf?" could be uttered as a request. But it is much harder to imagine cases in which "Is it the case that you at present have the ability to reach that book on the top shelf?" could be similarly used. Why?

I think the explanation for this fact may derive from another maxim of conversation having to do with speaking idiomatically. In general, if one speaks unidiomatically, hearers assume that there must be a special reason for it, and in consequence, various assumptions of normal speech are suspended. Thus, if I say, archaically, "Knowest thou him who calleth himself Richard Nixon?", you are not likely to respond as you would to an utterance of "Do you know Richard Nixon?"

Besides the maxims proposed by Grice, there seems to be an additional maxim of conversation that could be expressed as follows: "Speak idiomatically unless there is some special reason not to."[7] For this reason, the normal conversational assumptions on which the possibility of indirect speech acts rests are in large part suspended in the nonidiomatic cases.

The answer, then, to Problem 1 is in two parts. In order to be a plausible candidate at all for use as an indirect speech act, a sentence has to be idiomatic. But within the class of idiomatic sentences, some forms tend to become entrenched as conventional devices for indirect speech acts. In the case of

[7] This maxim could also be viewed as an extension of Grice's maxim of manner.

directives, in which politeness is the chief motivation for the indirect forms, certain forms are conventionally used as polite requests. Which kinds of forms are selected will, in all likelihood, vary from one language to another.

Problem 2: Why is there an asymmetry between the sincerity condition and the others such that one can perform an indirect request only by asserting the satisfaction of a sincerity condition, not by querying it, whereas one can perform indirect directives by either asserting or querying the satisfaction of the propositional content and preparatory conditions?

Thus, an utterance of "I want you to do it" can be a request, but not an utterance of "Do I want you to do it?" The former can take "please", the latter cannot. A similar asymmetry occurs in the case of reasons: "Do you want to leave us alone?" can be a request, but not "You want to leave us alone".[8] Again, the former can take "please", the latter cannot. How is one to explain these facts?

I believe the answer is that it is odd, in normal circumstances, to ask other people about the existence of one's own elementary psychological states, and odd to assert the existence of other people's elementary psychological states when addressing them. Since normally you are never in as good a position as I am to assert what I want, believe, intend, and so on, and since I am normally not in as good a position as you to assert what you want, believe, intend, and so on, it is, in general, odd for me to ask you about my states or tell you about yours. We shall see shortly that this asymmetry extends to the indirect performance of other kinds of speech acts.

Problem 3: Though this chapter is not intended as being about English syntactical forms, some of the sentences on our lists are of enough interest to deserve special comment. Even if it should turn out that these peculiar cases are really imperative idioms, like "how about ... ?", it would not alter the general lines of my argument; it would simply shift some

---

[8] This point does not hold for the etymologically prior sense of "want" in which it means "need".

examples out of the class of indirect speech acts into the class of imperative idioms.

One interesting form is "why not plus verb", as in "Why not stop here?" This form, unlike "Why don't you?", has many of the same syntactical constraints as imperative sentences. For example, it requires a voluntary verb. Thus, one cannot say *"Why not resemble your grandmother?" unless one believes that one can resemble someone as a voluntary action, whereas one can say "Why not imitate your grandmother?" Furthermore, like imperative sentences, this form requires a reflexive when it takes a second-person direct object, e.g. "Why not wash yourself?" Do these facts prove that the "Why not ... ?" (and the "why ... ?") forms are imperative in meaning? I think they are not. On my account, the way an utterance of "why not?" works is this: In asking "Why not stop here?" as a suggestion to stop here, *S* challenges *H* to provide reasons for not doing something on the tacit assumption that the absence of reasons for not doing something is itself a reason for doing it, and the suggestion to do it is therefore made indirectly in accordance with the generalization that alluding to a reason for doing something is a way of making an indirect directive to do it. This analysis is supported by several facts. First, as we have already seen, this form can have a literal utterance in which it is not uttered as a suggestion; second, one can respond to the suggestion with a response appropriate to the literal utterance, e.g., "Well, there are several reasons for not stopping here. First ...." And third, one can report an utterance of one of these, without reporting any directive illocutionary forces, in the form "He asked me why we shouldn't stop there." And here the occurrence of the practical "should" or "ought" (not the theoretical "should" or "ought") is sufficient to account for the requirement of a voluntary verb.

Other troublesome examples are provided by occurrences of "would" and "could" in indirect speech acts. Consider, for example, utterances of "Would you pass me the salt?" and "Could you hand me that book?" It is not easy to analyze these forms and to describe exactly how they differ in meaning from "Will you pass me the salt?" and "Can you hand me that book?" Where, for example, are we to find the "if" clause, which, we are sometimes told, is required by the so-called subjunctive use of these expressions? Suppose we treat the "if" clause as "if I asked you to". Thus, "Would you pass me the salt?" is short for "Would you pass me the salt if I asked you to?"

There are at least two difficulties with this approach. First, it does not seem at all plausible for "could", since your abilities and possibilities are not contingent on what I ask you to do. But second, even for "would" it is unsatisfactory, since "Would you pass me the salt if I asked you to?" does not have the same indirect illocutionary act potential as the simple "Would you pass me the salt?" Clearly, both forms have uses as indirect directives, but, equally clearly, they are not equivalent. Furthermore, the cases in which "would" and "could" interrogative forms *do* have a nonindirect use seem to be quite different from the cases we have been considering, e.g. "Would you vote for a Democrat?" or "Could you marry a radical?" Notice, for example, that an appropriate response to an utterance of these might be, e.g., "Under what conditions?" or "It depends on the situation". But these would hardly be appropriate responses to an utterance of "Would you pass me the salt?" in the usual dinner table scene we have been envisaging.

"Could" seems to be analyzable in terms of "would" and possibility or ability. Thus, "Could you marry a radical?" means something like "Would it be possible for you to marry a radical?" "Would", like "will" is traditionally analyzed either as expressing want or desire or as a future auxiliary.

The difficulty with these forms seems to be an instance of the general difficulty about the nature of the subjunctive and does not necessarily indicate that there is any imperative meaning. If we are to assume that "would" and "could" have an imperative meaning, then it seems we will be forced to assume, also, that they have a commissive meaning as well, since utterances of "Could I be of assistance?" and "Would you like some more wine?" are both normally offers. I find this conclusion implausible because it involves an unnecessary proliferation of meanings. It violates Occam's razor regarding concepts. It is more economical to assume that "could" and "would" are univocal in "Could you pass the salt?", "Could I be of assistance?", "Would you stop making that noise?", and "Would you like some more wine?" However, a really satisfactory analysis of these forms awaits a satisfactory analysis of the subjunctive. The most plausible analysis of the indirect request forms is that the suppressed "if" clause is the polite "if you please" or "if you will".

EXTENDING THE ANALYSIS

I want to conclude this chapter by showing that the general approach suggested in it will work for other types of indirection besides just directives. Obvious examples, often cited in the literature, are provided by the sincerity conditions. In general, one can perform any illocutionary act by asserting (though not by questioning) the satisfaction of the sincerity condition for that act. Thus, for example:

> I am sorry I did it (*an apology*).
> I think/believe he is in the next room (*an assertion*).
> I am so glad you won (*congratulations*).
> I intend to try harder next time, coach (*a promise*).
> I am grateful for your help (*thanks*).

I believe, however, that the richest mine for examples other than directives is provided by commissives, and a study of the examples of sentences used to perform indirect commissives (especially offers and promises) shows very much the same patterns that we found in the study of directives. Consider the following sentences, any of which can be uttered to perform an indirect offer (or, in some cases, a promise).

I. Sentences concerning the preparatory conditions:
  A. that S is able to perform the act:
     Can I help you?
     I can do that for you
     I could get it for you
     Could I be of assistance?

    B. that *H* wants *S* to perform the act:
        Would you like some help?
        Do you want me to go now, Sally?
        Wouldn't you like me to bring some more
            next time I come?
        Would you rather I came on Tuesday?
  II. Sentences concerning the sincerity condition:
        I intend to do it for you
        I plan on repairing it for you next week.
 III. Sentences concerning the propositional content condition:
        I will do it for you
        I am going to give it to you next time
            you stop by
        Shall I give you the money now?
  IV. Sentences concerning *S*'s wish or willingness to do *A*:
        I want to be of any help I can
        I'd be willing to do it (if you want me to).
   V. Sentences concerning (other) reasons for *S*'s doing *A*:
        I think I had better leave you alone
        Wouldn't it be better if I gave you some
            assistance?
        You need my help, Cynthia.

Notice that the point made earlier about the elementary psychological states holds for these cases as well: One can perform an indirect illocutionary act by asserting, but not by querying, one's own psychological states; and one can perform an indirect illocutionary act by querying, but not by asserting, the presence of psychological states in one's hearer.

Thus, an utterance of "Do you want me to leave?" can be an offer to leave, but not "You want me to leave." (Though it can be, with the tag question "You want me to leave, don't you?") Similarly, "I want to help you out" can be uttered as an offer, but not "Do I want to help you out?"

The class of indirect commissives also includes a large number of hypothetical sentences:

If you wish any further information, just
    let me know.

If I can be of assistance, I would be most
glad to help.
If you need any help, call me at the office.

In the hypothetical cases, the antecedent concerns either one
of the preparatory conditions, or the presence of a reason for
doing *A*, as in "If it would be better for me to come on
Wednesday, just let me know." Note also that, as well as
hypothetical sentences, there are iterated cases of indirection.
Thus, e.g., "I think I ought to help you out" can be uttered as
an indirect offer made by way of making an indirect assertion.
These examples suggest the following further generalizations:

*Generalization 5: S can make an indirect commissive by either
asking whether or stating that the preparatory condition concerning his
ability to do A obtains.*

*Generalization 6: S can make an indirect commissive by asking
whether, though not by stating that, the preparatory condition
concerning H's wish or want that S do A obtains.*

*Generalization 7: S can make an indirect commissive by stating
that, and in some forms by asking whether, the propositional content
condition obtains.*

*Generalization 8: S can make an indirect commissive by stating
that, but not by asking whether, the sincerity condition obtains.*

*Generalization 9: S can make an indirect commissive by stating
that or by asking whether there are good or overriding reasons for doing
A, except where the reason is that S wants or desires to do A, in
which case he can only state but not ask whether he wants to do A.*

I would like to conclude by emphasizing that my approach
does not fit any of the usual explanatory paradigms. The
philosopher's paradigm has normally been to get a set of
logically necessary and sufficient conditions for the phenomena to be explained; the linguist's paradigm has normally
been to get a set of structural rules that will generate the
phenomena to be explained. I am unable to convince myself
that either of these paradigms is appropriate for the present
problem. The problem seems to me somewhat like those
problems in the epistemological analysis of perception in
which one seeks to explain how a perceiver recognizes an

object on the basis of imperfect sensory input. The question, How do I know he has made a request when he only asked me a question about my abilities? may be like the question, How do I know it was a car when all I perceived was a flash going past me on the highway? If so, the answer to our problem may be neither "I have a set of axioms from which it can be deduced that he made a request" nor "I have a set of syntactical rules that generate an imperative deep structure for the sentence he uttered."

Chapter 3

THE LOGICAL STATUS OF
FICTIONAL DISCOURSE

I

I believe that speaking or writing in a language consists in performing speech acts of a quite specific kind called "illocutionary acts". These include making statements, asking questions, giving orders, making promises, apologizing, thanking, and so on. I also believe that there is a systematic set of relationships between the meanings of the words and sentences we utter and the illocutionary acts we perform in the utterance of those words and sentences.[1]

Now for anybody who holds such a view the existence of fictional discourse poses a difficult problem. We might put the problem in the form of a paradox: how can it be both the case that words and other elements in a fictional story have their ordinary meanings and yet the rules that attach to those words and other elements and determine their meanings are not complied with: how can it be the case in "Little Red Riding Hood" both that "red" means red and yet that the rules correlating "red" with red are not in force? This is only a preliminary formulation of our question and we shall have to attack the question more vigorously before we can even get a careful formulation of it. Before doing that, however, it is necessary to make a few elementary distinctions.

The distinction between fiction and literature: Some works of fiction are literary works, some are not. Nowadays most works of literature are fictional, but by no means all works of literature are fictional. Most comic books and jokes are examples of fiction but not literature; *In Cold Blood* and *Armies of the Night* qualify as literature but are not fictional.

[1] For an attempt to work out a theory of these relationships, see Searle (1969, esp. Chs. 3-5).

Because most literary works are fictional it is possible to confuse a definition of fiction with a definition of literature, but the existence of examples of fiction which are not literature and of examples of literature which are not fictional is sufficient to demonstrate that this is a mistake. And even if there were no such examples, it would still be a mistake because the concept of literature is a different concept from that of fiction. Thus, for example, "the Bible as literature" indicates a theologically neutral attitude, but "the Bible as fiction" is tendentious.[2]

In what follows I shall attempt to analyze the concept of fiction but not the concept of literature. Actually, in the same sense in which I shall be analyzing fiction, I do not believe it is possible to give an analysis of literature, for three interconnected reasons.

First, there is no trait or set of traits which all works of literature have in common and which could constitute the necessary and sufficient conditions for being a work of literature. Literature, to use Wittgenstein's terminology, is a family-resemblance notion.

Secondly, I believe (though will not attempt to demonstrate here) that "literature" is the name of a set of attitudes we take toward a stretch of discourse, not a name of an internal property of the stretch of discourse, though why we take the attitudes we do will of course be at least in part a function of the properties of the discourse and not entirely arbitrary. Roughly speaking, whether or not a work is literature is for the readers to decide, whether or not it is fiction is for the author to decide.

Third, the literary is continuous with the nonliterary. Not only is there no sharp boundary, but there is not much of a boundary at all. Thus Thucydides and Gibbon wrote works of history which we may or may not treat as works of literature. The Sherlock Holmes stories of Conan Doyle are

---

[2] There are other senses of "fiction" and "literature" which I will be discussing. In one sense "fiction" means falsehood, as in "The defendant's testimony was a tissue of fictions", and in one sense "literature" just means printed matter, as in "The literature on referential opacity is quite extensive."

clearly works of fiction, but it is a matter of judgment whether they should be regarded as a part of English literature.

The distinction between fictional speech and figurative speech: It is clear that just as in fictional speech semantic rules are altered or suspended in some way we have yet to analyze, so in figurative speech semantic rules are altered or suspended in some way. But it is equally clear that what happens in fictional speech is quite different from and independent of figures of speech. A metaphor can occur as much in a work of nonfiction as in a work of fiction. Just to have some jargon to work with, let us say that metaphorical uses of expressions are "nonliteral" and fictional utterances are "nonserious". To avoid one obvious sort of misunderstanding, this jargon is not meant to imply that writing a fictional novel or poem is not a serious activity, but rather that, for example, if the author of a novel tells us that it is raining outside he isn't seriously committed to the view that it is at the time of writing actually raining outside. It is in this sense that fiction is nonserious. Some examples: If I now say, "I am writing an article about the concept of fiction", that remark is both serious and literal. If I say, "Hegel is a dead horse on the philosophical market", that remark is serious but nonliteral. If I say, beginning a story, "Once upon a time there lived in a faraway Kingdom a wise King who had a beautiful daughter ..." that remark is literal but not serious.

The aim of this chapter is to explore the difference between fictional and serious utterances; it is not to explore the difference between figurative and literal utterances, which is another distinction quite independent of the first.

One last remark before we begin the analysis. Every subject matter has its catchphrases to enable us to stop thinking before we have got a solution to our problems. Just as sociologists and others who ponder social change find they can stop themselves from having to think by reciting phrases such as "the revolution of rising expectations", so it is easy to stop thinking about the logical status of fictional discourse if we repeat slogans like "the suspension of disbelief" or expressions like "mimesis". Such notions contain our problem but not its solution. In one sense I want to say precisely that what I do not suspend when I read a serious writer of nonserious illocutions such as Tolstoy or Thomas Mann is disbelief. My disbelief antennae are much more acute for Dostoevsky than they are for the *San Francisco Chronicle*. In another sense I do want to say that I "suspend disbelief", but our problem is to say exactly how and exactly why. Plato, according to one common misinterpretation, thought that fiction consisted of lies. Why would such a view be wrong?

II

Let us begin by comparing two passages chosen at random to illustrate the distinction between fiction and nonfiction. The first, nonfiction, is from the *New York Times* (December 15, 1972), written by Eileen Shanahan:

> Washington, Dec. 14 – A group of federal, state, and local government officials rejected today President Nixon's idea that the federal government provide the financial aid that would permit local governments to reduce property taxes.

The second is from a novel by Iris Murdoch entitled *The Red and the Green*, which begins,

> Ten more glorious days without horses! So thought Second Lieutenant Andrew Chase-White recently commissioned in the distinguished regiment of King Edward's Horse, as he pottered contentedly in a garden on the outskirts of Dublin on a sunny Sunday afternoon in April nineteen-sixteen.[3]

The first thing to notice about both passages is that, with the possible exception of the one word *pottered* in Miss Murdoch's novel, all of the occurrences of the words are quite literal. Both authors are speaking (writing) literally. What then are the differences? Let us begin by considering the

[3] Iris Murdoch, *The Red and the Green* (New York, 1965), p. 3. This and other examples of fiction used in this article were deliberately chosen at random, in the belief that theories of language should be able to deal with any text at all and not just with specially selected examples.

passage from the *New York Times*. Miss Shanahan is making an assertion. An assertion is a type of illocutionary act that conforms to certain quite specific semantic and pragmatic rules. These are:

1. The essential rule: the maker of an assertion commits himself to the truth of the expressed proposition.
2. The preparatory rules: the speaker must be in a position to provide evidence or reasons for the truth of the expressed proposition.
3. The expressed proposition must not be obviously true to both the speaker and the hearer in the context of utterance.
4. The sincerity rule: the speaker commits himself to a belief in the truth of the expressed proposition.[4]

Notice that Miss Shanahan is held responsible for complying with all these rules. If she fails to comply with any of them, we shall say that her assertion is defective. If she fails to meet the conditions specified by the rules, we will say that what she said is false or mistaken or wrong, or that she didn't have enough evidence for what she said, or that it was pointless because we all knew it anyhow, or that she was lying because she didn't really believe it. Such are the ways that assertions can characteristically go wrong, when the speaker fails to live up to the standards set by the rules. The rules establish the internal canons of criticism of the utterance.

But now notice that none of these rules apply to the passage from Miss Murdoch. Her utterance is not a commitment to the truth of the proposition that on a sunny Sunday afternoon in April of nineteen-sixteen a recently commissioned lieutenant of an outfit called the King Edward's Horse named Andrew Chase-White pottered in his garden and thought that he was going to have ten more glorious days without horses. Such a proposition may or may not be true, but Miss Murdoch has no commitment whatever

---

[4] For a more thorough exposition of these and similar rules, see Searle (1969), ch. 3.

as regards its truth. Furthermore, as she is not committed to its truth, she is not committed to being able to provide evidence for its truth. Again, there may or may not be evidence for the truth of such a proposition, and she may or may not have evidence. But all of that is quite irrelevant to her speech act, which does not commit her to the possession of evidence. Again, since there is no commitment to the truth of the proposition there is no question as to whether we are or are not already apprised of its truth, and she is not held to be insincere if in fact she does not believe for one moment that there actually was such a character thinking about horses that day in Dublin.

Now we come to the crux of our problem: Miss Shanahan is making an assertion, and assertions are defined by the constitutive rules of the activity of asserting; but what kind of illocutionary act can Miss Murdoch be performing? In particular, how can it be an assertion since it complies with none of the rules peculiar to assertions? If, as I have claimed, the meaning of the sentence uttered by Miss Murdoch is determined by the linguistic rules that attach to the elements of the sentence, and if those rules determine that the literal utterance of the sentence is an assertion, and if, as I have been insisting, she is making a literal utterance of the sentence, then surely it must be an assertion; but it can't be an assertion since it does not comply with those rules that are specific to and constitutive of assertions.

Let us begin by considering one wrong answer to our question, an answer which some authors have in fact proposed. According to this answer, Miss Murdoch or any other writer of novels is not performing the illocutionary act of making an assertion but the illocutionary act of telling a story or writing a novel. On this theory, newspaper accounts contain one class of illocutionary acts (statements, assertions, descriptions, explanations) and fictional literature contains another class of illocutionary acts (writing stories, novels, poems, plays, etc.). The writer or speaker of fiction has his own repertoire of illocutionary acts which are on all fours with, but in addition to, the standard illocutionary acts of asking questions, making requests, making promises, giving descriptions, and so on. I believe that this analysis is incorrect; I shall not devote a great deal of space to demonstrating that it is incorrect because I prefer to spend the space on presenting an alternative account, but by way of illustrating its incorrectness I want to mention a serious difficulty which anyone who wished to present such an account would face. In general the illocutionary act (or acts) performed in the utterance of the sentence is a function of the meaning of the sentence. We know, for example, that an utterance of the sentence "John can run the mile" is a performance of one kind of illocutionary act, and that an utterance of the sentence "Can John run the mile?" is a performance of another kind of illocutionary act, because we know that the indicative sentence form means something different from the interrogative sentence form. But now if the sentences in a work of fiction were used to perform some completely different speech acts from those determined by their literal meaning, they would have to have some other meaning. Anyone therefore who wishes to claim that fiction contains different illocutionary acts from nonfiction is committed to the view that words do not have their normal meanings in works of fiction. That view is at least *prima facie* an impossible view since if it were true it would be impossible for anyone to understand a work of fiction without learning a new set of meanings for all the words and other elements contained in the work of fiction, and since any sentence whatever can occur in a work of fiction, in order to have the ability to read any work of fiction, a speaker of the language would have to learn the language all over again, since every sentence in the language would have both a fictional and a nonfictional meaning. I can think of various ways that a defender of the view under consideration might meet these objections, but as they are all as unplausible as the original thesis that fiction contains some wholly new category of illocutionary acts, I shall not pursue them here.

Back to Miss Murdoch. If she is not performing the illocutionary act of writing a novel because there is no such illocutionary act, what exactly is she doing in the quoted passage? The answer seems to me obvious, though not easy to state precisely. She is pretending, one could say, to make an assertion, or acting as if she were making an assertion, or going through the motions of making an assertion, or imitating the making of an assertion. I place no great store by any of these verb phrases, but let us go to work on "pretend", as it is as good as any. When I say that Miss Murdoch is pretending to make an assertion, it is crucial to distinguish two quite different senses of "pretend". In one sense of "pretend", to pretend to be or to do something that one is not doing is to engage in a form of deception, but in the second sense of "pretend", to pretend to do or be something is to engage in a performance which is *as if* one were doing or being the thing and is without any intent to deceive. If I pretend to be Nixon in order to fool the Secret Service into letting me into the White House, I am pretending in the first sense; if I pretend to be Nixon as part of a game of charades, it is pretending in the second sense. Now in the fictional use of words, it is pretending in the second sense which is in question. Miss Murdoch is engaging in a nondeceptive pseudoperformance which constitutes pretending to recount to us a series of events. So my first conclusion is this: the author of a work of fiction pretends to perform a series of illocutionary acts, normally of the assertive type.[5]

Now *pretend* is an intentional verb: that is, it is one of those verbs which contain the concept of intention built into it. One cannot truly be said to have pretended to do something unless one intended to pretend to do it. So our first conclusion leads immediately to our second conclusion: the identifying criterion for whether or not a text is a work of fiction must of necessity lie in the illocutionary intentions of the author. There is no textual property, syntactical or semantic, that will identify a text as a work of fiction. What makes it a work of fiction is, so to speak, the illocutionary stance that the author takes toward it, and that stance is a

---

[5] The assertive class of illocutions includes statements, assertions, descriptions, characterizations, identifications, explanations, and numerous others. For an explanation of this and related notions see Searle (1975a, chapter 1 of this volume).

matter of the complex illocutionary intentions that the author has when he writes or otherwise composes it.

There used to be a school of literary critics who thought one should not consider the intentions of the author when examining a work of fiction. Perhaps there is some level of intention at which this extraordinary view is plausible; perhaps one should not consider an author's ulterior motives when analyzing his work, but at the most basic level it is absurd to suppose a critic can completely ignore the intentions of the author, since even so much as to identify a text as a novel, a poem, or even as a text is already to make a claim about the author's intentions.

So far I have pointed out that an author of fiction pretends to perform illocutionary acts which he is not in fact performing. But now the question forces itself upon us as to what makes this peculiar form of pretense possible. It is after all an odd, peculiar, and amazing fact about human language that it allows the possibility of fiction at all. Yet we all have no difficulty in recognizing and understanding works of fiction. How is such a thing possible?

In our discussion of Miss Shanahan's passage in the *New York Times*, we specified a set of rules, compliance with which makes her utterance a (sincere and nondefective) assertion. I find it useful to think of these rules as rules correlating words (or sentences) to the world. Think of them as vertical rules that establish connections between language and reality. Now what makes fiction possible, I suggest, is a set of extralinguistic, nonsemantic conventions that break the connection between words and the world established by the rules mentioned earlier. Think of the conventions of fictional discourse as a set of horizontal conventions that break the connections established by the vertical rules. They suspend the normal requirements established by these rules. Such horizontal conventions are not meaning rules; they are not part of the speaker's semantic competence. Accordingly, they do not alter or change the meanings of any of the words or other elements of the language. What they do rather is enable the speaker to use words with their literal meanings without undertaking the commitments that are normally required by those meanings. My third conclusion then is this: the pretended illocutions which constitute a work of fiction are made possible by the existence of a set of conventions which suspend the normal operation of the rules relating illocutionary acts and the world. In this sense, to use Wittgenstein's jargon, telling stories really is a separate language game; to be played it requires a separate set of conventions, though these conventions are not meaning rules; and the language game is not on all fours with illocutionary language games, but is parasitic on them.

This point will perhaps be clearer if we contrast fiction with lies. I think Wittgenstein was wrong when he said that lying is a language game that has to be learned like any other.[6] I think this is mistaken because lying consists in violating one of the regulative rules on the performance of speech acts, and any regulative rule at all contains within it the notion of a violation. Since the rule defines what constitutes a violation, it is not first necessary to learn to follow the rule and then learn a separate practice of breaking the rule. But in contrast, fiction is much more sophisticated than lying. To someone who did not understand the separate conventions of fiction, it would seem that fiction is merely lying. What distinguishes fiction from lies is the existence of a separate set of conventions which enables the author to go through the motions of making statements which he knows to be not true even though he has no intention to deceive.

We have discussed the question of what makes it possible for an author to use words literally and yet not be committed in accordance with the rules that attach to the literal meaning of those words. Any answer to that question forces the next question upon us: what are the mechanisms by which the author invokes the horizontal conventions – what procedures does he follow? If, as I have said, the author does not actually perform illocutionary acts but only pretends to, how is the pretense performed? It is a general feature of the concept of pretending that one can pretend to perform a higher order or complex action by *actually* performing lower

6 Wittgenstein (1953, par. 249).

order or less complex actions which are constitutive parts of the higher order or complex action. Thus, for example, one can pretend to hit someone by actually making the arm and fist movements that are characteristic of hitting someone. The hitting is pretended, but the movement of the arm and fist is real. Similarly, children pretend to drive a stationary car by actually sitting in the driver's seat, moving the steering wheel, pushing the gear shift lever, and so on. The same principle applies to the writing of fiction. The author pretends to perform illocutionary acts by way of actually uttering (writing) sentences. In the terminology of *Speech Acts*, the *illocutionary act* is pretended, but the *utterance act* is real. In Austin's terminology, the author pretends to perform *illocutionary acts* by way of actually performing *phonetic* and *phatic* acts. The utterance acts in fiction are indistinguishable from the utterance acts of serious discourse, and it is for that reason that there is no textual property that will identify a stretch of discourse as a work of fiction. It is the performance of the utterance act with the intention of invoking the horizontal conventions that constitutes the pretended performance of the illocutionary act.

The fourth conclusion of this section, then, is a development of the third: the pretended performances of illocutionary acts which constitute the writing of a work of fiction consist in actually performing utterance acts with the intention of invoking the horizontal conventions that suspend the normal illocutionary commitments of the utterances.

These points will be clearer if we consider two special cases of fiction, first-person narratives and theatrical plays. I have said that in the standard third-person narrative of the type exemplified by Miss Murdoch's novel, the author pretends to perform illocutionary acts. But now consider the following passage from Sherlock Holmes:

It was in the year '95 that a combination of events, into which I need not enter, caused Mr. Sherlock Holmes and myself to spend some weeks in one of our great university towns, and it was during this time that the small but instructive adventure which I am about to relate befell us.[7]

In this passage Sir Arthur is not simply pretending to make assertions, but he is *pretending to be* John Watson, MD, retired officer of the Afghan campaign making assertions about his friend Sherlock Holmes. That is, in first-person narratives, the author often pretends to be someone else making assertions.

Dramatic texts provide us with an interesting special case of the thesis I have been arguing in this chapter. Here it is not so much the author who is doing the pretending but the characters in the actual performance. That is, the text of the play will consist of some pseudoassertions, but it will for the most part consist of a series of serious directions to the actors as to how they are to pretend to make assertions and to perform other actions. The actor pretends to be someone other than he actually is, and he pretends to perform the speech acts and other acts of that character. The playwright represents the actual and pretended actions and the speeches of the actors, but the playwright's performance in writing the text of the play is rather like writing a recipe for pretense than engaging in a form of pretense itself. A fictional story is a pretended representation of a state of affairs; but a play, that is, a play as performed, is not a pretended *representation* of a state of affairs but the pretended state of affairs itself, the actors pretend *to be* the characters. In that sense the author of the play is not in general pretending to make assertions; he is giving directions as to how to enact a pretense which the actors then follow. Consider the following passage from Galsworthy's *The Silver Box*:

> Act I, Scene I. The curtain rises on the Barthwicks' dining room, large, modern, and well furnished; the window curtains drawn. Electric light is burning. On the large round dining table is set out a tray with whiskey, a syphon, and a silver cigarette box. It is past midnight. A fumbling is heard outside the door. It is opened suddenly; Jack Barthwick seems to fall into the room . . .

[7] A. Conan Doyle, *The Complete Sherlock Holmes* (Garden City, NY, 1932), II, 596.

Jack: Hello! I've got home all ri--- (*Defiantly*.)[8]

It is instructive to compare this passage with Miss Murdoch's. Murdoch, I have claimed, tells us a story; in order to do that, she pretends to make a series of assertions about people in Dublin in 1916. What we visualize when we read the passage is a man pottering about his garden thinking about horses. But when Galsworthy writes his play, he does not give us a series of pretended assertions about a play. He gives us a series of directions as to how things are actually to happen on stage when the play is performed. When we read the passage from Galsworthy we visualize a stage, the curtain rises, the stage is furnished like a dining room, and so on. That is, it seems to me the illocutionary force of the text of a play is like the illocutionary force of a recipe for baking a cake. It is a set of instructions for how to do something, namely, how to perform the play. The element of pretense enters at the level of the performance: the actors pretend to be the members of the Barthwick family doing such-and-such things and having such-and-such feelings.

III

The analysis of the preceding section, if it is correct, should help us to solve some of the traditional puzzles about the ontology of a work of fiction. Suppose I say: "There never existed a Mrs. Sherlock Holmes because Holmes never got married, but there did exist a Mrs. Watson because Watson did get married, though Mrs. Watson died not long after their marriage." Is what I have said true or false, or lacking in truth value, or what? In order to answer we need to distinguish not only between serious discourse and fictional discourse, as I have been doing, but also to distinguish both of these from serious discourse about fiction. Taken as a piece of serious discourse, the above passage is certainly not true because none of these people (Watson, Holmes, Mrs. Watson) ever existed. But taken as a piece of discourse *about* fiction, the

---

[8] John Galsworthy, *Representative Plays* (New York, 1924), p. 3.

above statement is true because it accurately reports the marital histories of the two fictional characters Holmes and Watson. It is not itself a piece of fiction because I am not the author of the works of fiction in question. Holmes and Watson never existed at all, which is not of course to deny that they exist in fiction and can be talked about as such.

Taken as a statement about fiction, the above utterance conforms to the constitutive rules of statement-making. Notice, for example, that I can verify the above statement by reference to the works of Conan Doyle. But there is no question of Conan Doyle being able to verify what he says about Sherlock Holmes and Watson when he writes the stories, because he does not make any statements about them, he only pretends to. Because the author has created these fictional characters, we on the other hand can make true statements about them as fictional characters.

But how is it possible for an author to "create" fictional characters out of thin air, as it were? To answer this let us go back to the passage from Iris Murdoch. The second sentence begins, "So thought Second Lieutenant Andrew Chase-White". Now in this passage Murdoch uses a proper name, a paradigm referring expression. Just as in the whole sentence she pretends to make an assertion, in this passage she pretends to refer (another speech act). One of the conditions on the successful performance of the speech act of reference is that there must exist an object that the speaker is referring to. Thus by pretending to refer she pretends that there is an object to be referred to. To the extent that we share in the pretense, we will also pretend that there is a lieutenant named Andrew Chase-White living in Dublin in 1916. It is the pretended reference which creates the fictional character and the shared pretense which enables us to talk about the character in the manner of the passage about Sherlock Holmes quoted above. The logical structure of all this is complicated, but it is not opaque. By pretending to refer to (and recount the adventures of) a person, Miss Murdoch creates a fictional character. Notice that she does not really refer to a fictional character because there was no such antecedently existing character; rather, by pretending to refer to a person she creates a fictional person. Now once that fictional character has been created, we who are standing outside the fictional story can really refer to a fictional person. Notice that in the passage about Sherlock Holmes above, I really referred to a fictional character (i.e., my utterance satisfies the rules of reference). I did not *pretend* to refer to a real Sherlock Holmes; I *really referred* to the fictional Sherlock Holmes.

Another interesting feature of fictional reference is that normally not all of the references in a work of fiction will be pretended acts of referring; some will be real references as in the passage from Miss Murdoch where she refers to Dublin, or in Sherlock Holmes when Conan Doyle refers to London, or in the passage quoted when he makes a veiled reference to either Oxford or Cambridge but doesn't tell us which ("one of our great university towns"). Most fictional stories contain nonfictional elements: along with the pretended references to Sherlock Holmes and Watson, there are in Sherlock Holmes real references to London and Baker Street and Paddington Station; again, in *War and Peace*, the story of Pierre and Natasha is a fictional story about fictional characters, but the Russia of *War and Peace* is the real Russia, and the war against Napoleon is the real war against the real Napoleon. What is the test for what is fictional and what isn't? The answer is provided by our discussion of the differences between Miss Murdoch's novel and Miss Shanahan's article in the *New York Times*. The test for what the author is committed to is what counts as a mistake. If there never did exist a Nixon, Miss Shanahan (and the rest of us) are mistaken. But if there never did exist an Andrew Chase-White, Miss Murdoch is not mistaken. Again, if Sherlock Holmes and Watson go from Baker Street to Paddington Station by a route which is geographically impossible, we will know that Conan Doyle blundered even though he has not blundered if there never was a veteran of the Afghan campaign answering to the description of John Watson, MD. In part, certain fictional genres are defined by the nonfictional commitments involved in the work of fiction. The difference, say, between naturalistic novels, fairy stories, works of science fiction, and surrealistic stories is in part defined by the extent of the author's commitment to represent actual facts, either specific facts about places like London and Dublin and Russia or general facts about what it is possible for people to do and what the world is like. For example, if Billy Pilgrim makes a trip to the invisible planet Tralfamadore in a microsecond, we can accept that because it is consistent with the science fiction element of *Slaughterhouse Five*, but if we find a text where Sherlock Holmes does the same thing, we will know at the very least that that text is inconsistent with the corpus of the original nine volumes of the Sherlock Holmes stories.

Theorists of literature are prone to make vague remarks about how the author creates a fictional world, a world of the novel, or some such. I think we are now in a position to make sense of those remarks. By pretending to refer to people and to recount events about them, the author creates fictional characters and events. In the case of realistic or naturalistic fiction, the author will refer to real places and events intermingling these references with the fictional references, thus making it possible to treat the fictional story as an extension of our existing knowledge. The author will establish with the reader a set of understandings about how far the horizontal conventions of fiction break the vertical connections of serious speech. To the extent that the author is consistent with the conventions he has invoked or (in the case of revolutionary forms of literature) the conventions he has established, he will remain within the conventions. As far as the *possibility* of the ontology is concerned, anything goes: the author can create any character or event he likes. As far as the *acceptability* of the ontology is concerned, coherence is a crucial consideration. However, there is no universal criterion for coherence: what counts as coherence in a work of science fiction will not count as coherence in a work of naturalism. What counts as coherence will be in part a function of the contract between author and reader about the horizontal conventions.

Sometimes the author of a fictional story will insert utterances in the story which are not fictional and not part of the story. To take a famous example, Tolstoy begins *Anna Karenina* with the sentence "Happy families are all happy in the same way, unhappy families unhappy in their separate, different ways." That, I take it, is not a fictional but a serious utterance. It is a genuine assertion. It is part of the novel but not part of the fictional story. When Nabokov at the beginning of *Ada* deliberately misquotes Tolstoy, saying, "All happy families are more or less dissimilar; all unhappy ones more or less alike", he is indirectly contradicting (and poking fun at) Tolstoy. Both of these are genuine assertions, though Nabokov's is made by an ironic misquotation of Tolstoy. Such examples compel us to make a final distinction, that between a work of fiction and fictional discourse. A work of fiction need not consist entirely of, and in general will not consist entirely of, fictional discourse.

IV

The preceding analysis leaves one crucial question un-answered: why bother? That is, why do we attach such importance and effort to texts which contain largely pretended speech acts? The reader who has followed my argument this far will not be surprised to hear that I do not think there is any simple or even single answer to that question. Part of the answer would have to do with the crucial role, usually underestimated, that imagination plays in human life, and the equally crucial role that shared products of the imagination play in human social life. And one aspect of the role that such products play derives from the fact that serious (i.e. nonfictional) speech acts can be conveyed by fictional texts, even though the conveyed speech act is not represented in the text. Almost any important work of fiction conveys a "message" or "messages" which are conveyed *by* the text but are not *in* the text. Only in such children's stories as contain the concluding "and the moral of the story is ..." or in tiresomely didactic authors such as Tolstoy do we get an explicit representation of the serious speech acts which it is the point (or the main point) of the fictional text to convey. Literary critics have explained on an ad hoc and particularistic basis how the author conveys a serious speech act through the performance of the pretended speech acts which constitute the work of fiction, but there is as yet no general theory of the mechanisms by which such serious illocutionary intentions are conveyed by pretended illocutions.

Chapter 4

METAPHOR

FORMULATING THE PROBLEM

If you hear somebody say, "Sally is a block of ice", or "Sam is a pig", you are likely to assume that the speaker does not mean what he says literally, but that he is speaking metaphorically. Furthermore, you are not likely to have very much trouble figuring out what he means. If he says, "Sally is a prime number between 17 and 23", or "Bill is a barn door", you might still assume he is speaking metaphorically, but it is much harder to figure out what he means. The existence of such utterances – utterances in which the speaker means metaphorically something different from what the sentence means literally – poses a series of questions for any theory of language and communication: What is metaphor, and how does it differ from both literal and other forms of figurative utterances? Why do we use expressions metaphorically instead of saying exactly and literally what we mean? How do metaphorical utterances work, that is, how is it possible for speakers to communicate to hearers when speaking meta-phorically inasmuch as they do not say what they mean? And why do some metaphors work and others not?

In my discussion, I propose to tackle this latter set of questions – those centering around the problem of how metaphors work – both because of its intrinsic interest, and because it does not seem to me that we shall get an answer to the others until this fundamental question has been answered. Before we can begin to understand it, however, we need to formulate the question more precisely.

The problem of explaining how metaphors work is a special case of the general problem of explaining how speaker's meaning and sentence or word meaning come apart. It is a special case, that is, of the problem of how it is possible to say one thing and mean something else, occasions where one succeeds in communicating what one means even though both the speaker and the hearer know that the meanings of the words uttered by the speaker do not exactly and literally express what the speaker meant. Some other instances of the break between speaker's utterance meaning and literal sentence meaning are irony and indirect speech acts. In each of these cases, what the speaker means is not identical with what the sentence means, and yet what he means is in various ways dependent on what the sentence means.

It is essential to emphasize at the very beginning that the problem of metaphor concerns the relations between word and sentence meaning, on the one hand, and speaker's meaning or utterance meaning, on the other. Many writers on the subject try to locate the metaphorical element of a metaphorical utterance in the sentence or expressions uttered. They think there are two kinds of sentence meaning, literal and metaphorical. However, sentences and words have only the meanings that they have. Strictly speaking, whenever we talk about the metaphorical meaning of a word, expression, or sentence, we are talking about what a speaker might utter it to mean, in a way that departs from what the word, expression, or sentence actually means. We are, therefore, talking about possible speaker's intentions. Even when we discuss how a nonsense sentence, such as Chomsky's example, "Colorless green ideas sleep furiously", could be given a metaphorical interpretation, what we are talking about is how a speaker could utter the sentence and mean something by it metaphorically, even though it is literally nonsensical. To have a brief way of distinguishing what a speaker means by uttering words, sentences, and expressions, on the one hand, and what the words, sentences, and expressions mean, on the other, I shall call the former *speaker's utterance meaning,* and the latter, *word, or sentence, meaning.* Metaphorical meaning is always speaker's utterance meaning.

In order that the speaker can communicate using metaphorical utterances, ironical utterances, and indirect speech acts, there must be some principles according to which he is able to mean more than, or something different from, what he says – principles known to the hearer, who, using this knowledge, can understand what the speaker means. The relation between the sentence meaning and the metaphorical utterance meaning is systematic rather than random or ad hoc. Our task in constructing a theory of metaphor is to try to state the principles which relate literal sentence meaning to metaphorical utterance meaning. Because the knowledge that enables people to use and understand metaphorical utterances goes beyond their knowledge of the literal meanings of words and sentences, the principles we seek are not included, or at least not entirely included, within a theory of semantic competence as traditionally conceived. From the point of view of the hearer, the problem of a theory of metaphor is to explain how he can understand the speaker's utterance meaning given that all he hears is a sentence with its word and sentence meaning. From the point of view of the speaker, the problem is to explain how he can mean something different from the word and sentence meaning of the sentence he utters. In the light of these reflections, our original question, How do metaphors work? can be recast as follows: What are the principles that enable speakers to formulate, and hearers to understand, metaphorical utterances? and How can we state these principles in a way that makes it clear how metaphorical utterances differ from other sorts of utterances in which speaker meaning does not coincide with literal meaning?

Because part of our task is to explain how metaphorical utterances differ from literal utterances, to start with we must arrive at a characterization of literal utterances. Most – indeed all – of the authors I have read on the subject of metaphor assume that we know how literal utterances work; they do not think that the problem of literal utterances is worth discussing in their account of metaphor. The price they pay for this is that their accounts often describe metaphorical utterances in ways that fail to distinguish them from literal ones.

In fact, to give an accurate account of literal predication is an extremely difficult, complex, and subtle problem. I shall not attempt anything like a thorough summary of the principles of literal utterance but shall remark on only those features which are essential for a comparison of literal utterance with metaphorical utterance. Also, for the sake of simplicity, I shall confine most of my discussion of both literal and metaphorical utterance to very simple cases, and to sentences used for the speech act of assertion.

Imagine that a speaker makes a literal utterance of a sentence such as

1. Sally is tall
2. The cat is on the mat
3. It's getting hot in here.

Now notice that, in each of these cases, the literal meaning of the sentence determines, at least in part, a set of truth conditions; and because the only illocutionary force indicating devices (see Searle, 1969) in the sentences are assertive, the literal and serious utterance of one of these sentences will commit the speaker to the existence of the set of truth conditions determined by the meaning of that sentence, together with the other determinants of truth conditions. Notice, furthermore, that in each case the sentence only determines a definite set of truth conditions relative to a particular context. That is because each of these examples has some indexical element, such as the present tense, or the demonstrative "here", or the occurrence of contextually dependent definite descriptions, such as "the cat" and "the mat".

In these examples, the contextually dependent elements of the sentence are explicitly realized in the semantic structure of the sentence: One can see and hear the indexical expressions. But these sentences, like most sentences, only determine a set of truth conditions against a background of assumptions that are not explicitly realized in the semantic structure of the sentence. This is most obvious for 1 and 3, because they contain the relative terms "tall" and "hot". These are what old-fashioned grammarians called "attributive" terms, and they only determine a definite set of truth conditions against a background of factual assumptions about the sort of things referred to by the speaker in the rest of the sentence. Moreover, these assumptions are not explicitly realized in the semantic structure of the sentence. Thus, a woman can be correctly described as "tall" even though she is shorter than a giraffe that could correctly be described as "short".

Though this dependence of the application of the literal meaning of the sentence on certain factual background assumptions that are not part of the literal meaning is most obvious for sentences containing attributive terms, the phenomenon is quite general. Sentence 2 only determines a definite set of truth conditions given certain assumptions about cats, mats, and the relation of being on. However, these assumptions are not part of the semantic content of the sentence. Suppose, for example, that the cat and mat are in the usual cat-on-mat spatial configuration, only both cat and mat are in outer space, outside any gravitational field relative to which one could be said to be "above" or "over" the other. Is the cat still *on* the mat? Without some further assumptions, the sentence does not determine a definite set of truth conditions in this context. Or suppose all cats suddenly became lighter than air, and the cat went flying about with the mat stuck to its belly. Is the cat still on the mat?

We know without hesitation what are the truth conditions of, "The fly is on the ceiling", but not of, "The cat is on the ceiling," and this difference is not a matter of meaning, but a matter of how our factual background information enables us to apply the meanings of sentences. In general, one can say that in most cases a sentence only determines a set of truth conditions relative to a set of assumptions that are not realized in the semantic content of the sentence. Thus, even in literal utterances, where speaker's meaning coincides with sentence meaning, the speaker must contribute more to the literal utterance than just the semantic content of the sentence, because that semantic content only determines a set of truth conditions relative to a set of assumptions made by the speaker, and if communication is to be successful his assumptions must be shared by the hearer. (For further discussion on this point, see Searle, 1978, chapter 5 of this volume.)

Notice finally that the notion of similarity plays a crucial role in any account of literal utterance. This is because the literal meaning of any general term, by determining a set of truth conditions, also determines a criterion of similarity between objects. To know that a general term is true of a set of objects is to know that they are similar with respect to the property specified by that term. All tall women are similar with respect to being tall, all hot rooms similar with respect to being hot, all square objects similar with respect to being square, and so on.

To summarize this brief discussion of some aspects of literal utterance, there are three features we shall need to keep in mind in our account of metaphorical utterance. First, in literal utterance the speaker means what he says; that is, literal sentence meaning and speaker's utterance meaning are the same; second, in general the literal meaning of a sentence only determines a set of truth conditions relative to a set of background assumptions which are not part of the semantic content of the sentence; and third, the notion of similarity plays an essential role in any account of literal predication.

When we turn to cases where utterance meaning and sentence meaning are different, we find them quite various. Thus, for example, 3 could be uttered not only to tell somebody that it is getting hot in the place of utterance (literal utterance), but it could also be used to request somebody to open a window (indirect speech act), to complain about how cold it is (ironical utterance), or to remark on the increasing vituperation of an argument that is in progress (metaphorical utterance). In our account of metaphorical utterance, we shall need to distinguish it not only from literal utterance, but also from these other forms in which literal utterance is departed from, or exceeded, in some way.

Because in metaphorical utterances what the speaker means differs from what he says (in one sense of "say"), in general we shall need two sentences for our examples of metaphor – first the sentence uttered metaphorically, and second a sentence that expresses literally what the speaker means when he utters the first sentence and means it metaphorically. Thus 3, the metaphor (MET):

3. (MET) It's getting hot in here

corresponds to 3, the paraphrase (PAR):

3. (PAR) The argument that is going on is becoming more vituperative

and similarly with the pairs:

4. (MET) Sally is a block of ice
4. (PAR) Sally is an extremely unemotional and unresponsive person
5. (MET) I have climbed to the top of the greasy pole (Disraeli)
5. (PAR) I have after great difficulty become prime minister
6. (MET) Richard is a gorilla
6. (PAR) Richard is fierce, nasty, and prone to violence.

Notice that in each case we feel that the paraphrase is somehow inadequate, that something is lost. One of our tasks will be to explain this sense of dissatisfaction that we have with paraphrases of even feeble metaphors. Still, in some sense, the paraphrases must approximate what the speaker meant, because in each case the speaker's metaphorical assertion will be true if, and only if, the corresponding assertion using the "PAR" sentence is true. When we get to more elaborate examples, our sense of the inadequacy of the paraphrase becomes more acute. How would we paraphrase

7. (MET) My Life had stood – a Loaded Gun –
   In Corners – till a Day
   The Owner passed – identified –
   And carried Me away – (Emily Dickinson)?

Clearly a good deal is lost by

7. (PAR) My life was one of unrealized but readily realizable potential (a loaded gun) in mediocre surroundings (corners) until such time (a day) when my destined lover (the owner) came (passed),

recognized my potential (identified), and took (carried) me away.

Yet, even in this case, the paraphrase or something like it must express a large part of speaker's utterance meaning, because the truth conditions are the same.

Sometimes we feel that we know exactly what the metaphor means and yet would not be able to formulate a literal "PAR" sentence because there are no literal expressions that convey what it means. Thus even for such a simple case as

8.   (MET) The ship ploughed the sea,

we may not be able to construct a simple paraphrase sentence even though there is no obscurity in the metaphorical utterance. And indeed metaphors often serve to plug such semantic gaps as this. In other cases, there may be an indefinite range of paraphrases. For example, when Romeo says:

9.   (MET) Juliet is the sun,

there may be a range of things he might mean. But while lamenting the inadequacy of paraphrases, let us also recall that paraphrase is a symmetrical relation. To say that the paraphrase is a poor paraphrase of the metaphor is also to say that the metaphor is a poor paraphrase of its paraphrase. Furthermore, we should not feel apologetic about the fact that some of our examples are trite or dead metaphors. Dead metaphors are especially interesting for our study, because, to speak oxymoronically, dead metaphors have lived on. They have become dead through continual use, but their continual use is a clue that they satisfy some semantic need.

Confining ourselves to the simplest subject–predicate cases, we can say that the general form of the metaphorical utterance is that a speaker utters a sentence of the form "S is P" and means metaphorically that S is R. In analyzing metaphorical predication, we need to distinguish, therefore, between three sets of elements. Firstly, there is the subject expression "S" and the object or objects it is used to refer to.

Secondly, there is the predicate expression "*P*" that is uttered and the literal meaning of that expression with its corresponding truth conditions, plus the denotation if there is any. And thirdly, there is the speaker's utterance meaning "*S* is *R*" and the truth conditions determined by that meaning. In its simplest form, the problem of metaphor is to try to get a characterization of the relations between the three sets, *S*, *P*, and *R*,[1] together with a specification of other information and principles used by speakers and hearers, so as to explain how it is possible to utter "*S* is *P*" and mean "*S* is *R*", and how it is possible to communicate that meaning from speaker to hearer. Now, obviously, that is not all there is to understand about metaphorical utterances; the speaker does more than just assert that *S* is *R*, and the peculiar effectiveness of metaphor will have to be explained in terms of how he does more than just assert that *S* is *R* and why he should choose this roundabout way of asserting that *S* is *R* in the first place. But at this stage we are starting at the beginning. At the very minimum, a theory of metaphor must explain how it is possible to utter "*S* is *P*" and both mean and communicate that *S* is *R*.

We can now state one of the differences between literal and metaphorical utterances as applied to these simple examples: In the case of literal utterance, speaker's meaning and sentence meaning are the same; therefore the assertion made about the object referred to will be true if and only if it satisfies the truth conditions determined by the meaning of the general term as applied against a set of shared background assumptions. In order to understand the utterance, the hearer does not require any extra knowledge beyond his knowledge of the rules of language, his awareness of the conditions of utterance, and a set of shared background assumptions. But, in the case of the metaphorical utterance, the truth conditions of the assertion are not determined by the truth conditions of the sentence and its

---

[1] It is essential to avoid any use–mention confusions when talking about these sets. Sometimes we will be talking about the words, other times about meanings, other times about references and denotations, and still other times about truth conditions.

general term. In order to understand the metaphorical utterance, the hearer requires something more than his knowledge of the language, his awareness of the conditions of the utterance, and background assumptions that he shares with the speaker. He must have some other principles, or some other factual information, or some combination of principles and information that enables him to figure out that when the speaker says, "*S* is *P*", he means "*S* is *R*". What is this extra element?

I believe that, at the most general level, the question has a fairly simple answer, but it will take me much of the rest of this discussion to work it out in any detail. The basic principle on which all metaphor works is that the utterance of an expression with its literal meaning and corresponding truth conditions can, in various ways that are specific to metaphor, call to mind another meaning and corresponding set of truth conditions. The hard problem of the theory of metaphor is to explain what exactly are the principles according to which the utterance of an expression can metaphorically call to mind a different set of truth conditions from the one determined by its literal meaning, and to state those principles precisely and without using metaphorical expressions like "call to mind".

SOME COMMON MISTAKES ABOUT METAPHOR

Before attempting to sketch a theory of metaphor, I want in this section and the next to backtrack a bit and examine some existing theories. Roughly speaking, theories of metaphor from Aristotle to the present can be divided into two types.[2] Comparison theories assert that metaphorical utterances involve a *comparison* or *similarity* between two or more *objects* (e.g. Aristotle; Henle, 1965), and semantic interaction theories claim that metaphor involves a *verbal opposition* (Beardsley, 1962) or *interaction* (Black, 1962) between two *semantic contents*, that of the expression used metaphorically, and that of the surrounding literal context. I think that both

[2] I follow Beardsley (1962) in this classification.

of these theories, if one tries to take them quite literally, are in various ways inadequate; nonetheless, they are both trying to say something true, and we ought to try to extract what is true in them. But first I want to show some of the common mistakes they contain and some further common mistakes made in discussions of metaphor. My aim here is not polemical; rather, I am trying to clear the ground for the development of a theory of metaphor. One might say the endemic vice of the comparison theories is that they fail to distinguish between the claim that the statement of the comparison is part of the *meaning*, and hence the *truth conditions* of the metaphorical statement, and the claim that the statement of the similarity is the *principle of inference*, or a step in the process of *comprehending*, on the basis of which speakers produce and hearers understand metaphor. (More about this distinction later.) The semantic interaction theories were developed in response to the weaknesses of the comparison theories, and they have little independent argument to recommend them other than the weakness of their rivals: Their endemic vice is the failure to appreciate the distinction between sentence or word meaning, which is never metaphorical, and speaker or utterance meaning, which can be metaphorical. They usually try to locate metaphorical meaning in the sentence or some set of associations with the sentence. In any event, here are half a dozen mistakes which I believe should be noted:

It is often said that in metaphorical utterances there is a change in meaning of at least one expression. I wish to say that on the contrary, strictly speaking, in metaphor there is never a change of meaning; diachronically speaking, metaphors do indeed initiate semantic changes, but to the extent that there has been a genuine change in meaning, so that a word or expression no longer means what it previously did, to precisely that extent the locution is no longer metaphorical. We are all familiar with the processes whereby an expression becomes a dead metaphor, and then finally becomes an idiom or acquires a new meaning different from the original meaning. But in a genuine metaphorical utterance, it is only because the expressions have not changed their meaning that there is a metaphorical utterance at all. The people who make this claim seem to be confusing *sentence* meaning with *speaker's* meaning. The metaphorical utterance does indeed mean something different from the meaning of the words and sentences, but that is not because there has been any change in the meanings of the lexical elements, but because the speaker means something different by them; speaker meaning does not coincide with sentence or word meaning. It is essential to see this point, because the main problem of metaphor is to explain how speaker meaning and sentence meaning are different and how they are, nevertheless, related. Such an explanation is impossible if we suppose that sentence or word meaning has changed in the metaphorical utterance.

The simplest way to show that the crude versions of the comparison view are false is to show that, in the production and understanding of metaphorical utterances, there need not be any two objects for comparison. When I say metaphorically

4.   (MET) Sally is a block of ice,

I am not necessarily quantifying over blocks of ice at all. My utterance does not entail literally that

10. $(\exists x)$ (x is a block of ice),

and such that I am comparing Sally to x. This point is even more obvious if we take expressions used as metaphors which have a null extension. If I say

11.   Sally is a dragon

that does not entail literally

12. $(\exists x)$ (x is a dragon).

Or, another way to see the same thing is to note that the negative utterance is just as metaphorical as the affirmative. If I say

13.   Sally is not a block of ice,

that, I take it, does not invite the absurd question: Which

block of ice is it that you are comparing Sally with, in order to say that she is not like it? At its *crudest*, the comparison theory is just muddled about the referential character of expressions used metaphorically.

Now, this might seem a somewhat minor objection to the comparison theorists, but it paves the way for a much more radical objection. Comparison theories which are explicit on the point at all, generally treat the statement of the comparison as part of the meaning and hence as part of the truth conditions of the metaphorical statement. For example, Miller (1979) is quite explicit in regarding metaphorical statements as statements of similarity, and indeed for such theorists the meaning of a *metaphorical* statement is always given by an explicit *statement* of similarity. Thus, in their view, I have not even formulated the problem correctly. According to me, the problem of explaining (simple subject – predicate) metaphors is to explain how the speaker and hearer go from the literal sentence meaning "*S* is *P*" to the metaphorical utterance meaning "*S* is *R*". But, according to them, that is not the utterance meaning; rather the utterance meaning must be expressible by an explicit statement of similarity, such as "*S* is like *P* with respect to *R*", or in Miller's case, the metaphorical statement "*S* is *P*" is to be analyzed as, "There is some property *F* and some property *G* such that *S*'s being *F* is similar to *P*'s being *G*". I will have more to say about this thesis and its exact formulation later, but at present I want to claim that though similarity often plays a role in the *comprehension* of metaphor, the metaphorical assertion is not necessarily an *assertion* of similarity. The simplest argument that metaphorical assertions are not always assertions of similarity is that given above: there are true metaphorical assertions for which there are no objects to be designated by the *P* term, hence the true metaphorical statement cannot falsely presuppose the existence of an object of comparison. But even where there are objects of comparison, the metaphorical assertion is not necessarily an assertion of similarity. Similarity, I shall argue, has to do with the production and understanding of metaphor, not with its meaning.

A second simple argument to show that metaphorical assertions are not necessarily assertions of similarity is that often the metaphorical assertion can remain true even though it turns out that the statement of similarity on which the inference to the metaphorical meaning is based is false. Thus, suppose I say,

6. (MET) Richard is a gorilla

meaning

6. (PAR) Richard is fierce, nasty, prone to violence, and so forth.

And suppose the hearer's inference to 6 (PAR) is based on the belief that

14. Gorillas are fierce, nasty, prone to violence, and so forth,

and hence 6 (MET) and 14, on the comparison view, would justify the inference to

15. Richard and gorillas are similar in several respects; *viz.*, they are fierce, nasty, prone to violence, and so forth

and this in turn would be part of the inference pattern that enabled the hearer to conclude that when I uttered 6 (MET) I meant 6 (PAR). But suppose ethological investigation shows, as I am told it has, that gorillas are not at all fierce and nasty, but are in fact shy, sensitive creatures, given to bouts of sentimentality. This would definitely show that 15 is false, for 15 is as much an assertion about gorillas as about Richard. But would it show that when I uttered 6 (MET), what I said was false? Clearly not, for what I meant was 6 (PAR), and 6 (PAR) is an assertion about Richard. It can remain true regardless of the actual facts about gorillas; though, of course, what expressions we use to convey metaphorically certain semantic contents will normally depend on what we take the facts to be.

To put it crudely, "Richard is a gorilla", is just about Richard; it is not literally about gorillas at all. The word "gorilla" here serves to convey a certain semantic content other than its own meaning by a set of principles I have yet to state. But 15 is literally about both Richard and gorillas, and it is true if and only if they both share the properties it claims they do. Now, it may well be true that the hearer employs something like 15 as a step in the procedures that get him from 6 (MET) to 6 (PAR), but it does not follow from this fact about his *procedures of comprehension* that this is part of the *speaker's utterance meaning* of 6 (MET); and, indeed, that it is not part of the utterance meaning is shown by the fact that the metaphorical statement can be *true* even if it turns out that gorillas do not have the traits that the metaphorical occurrence of "gorilla" served to convey. I am not saying that a metaphorical assertion can *never* be equivalent in meaning to a statement of similarity – whether or not it is would depend on the intentions of the speaker, but I am saying that it is not a necessary feature of metaphor – and is certainly not the point of having metaphor – that metaphorical assertions are equivalent in meaning to statements of similarity. My argument is starkly simple: In many cases the metaphorical statement and the corresponding similarity statement cannot be equivalent in meaning because they have different truth conditions. The difference between the view I am attacking and the one I shall espouse is this. According to the view I am attacking, 6 (MET) *means* Richard and gorillas are similar in certain respects. According to the view I shall espouse, similarity functions as a comprehension strategy, not as a component of meaning: 6 (MET) says that Richard has certain traits (and to figure out what they are, look for features associated with gorillas). On my account the *P* term need not figure literally in the statement of the truth conditions of the metaphorical statement at all.

Similar remarks apply incidentally to similes. If I say,

16. Sam acts like a gorilla

that need not commit me to the truth of

17. Gorillas are such that their behaviour resembles Sam's.

For 16 need not be about gorillas at all, and we might say that "gorilla" in 16 has a metaphorical occurrence. Perhaps this is one way we might distinguish between figurative similes and literal statements of similarity. Figurative similes need not necessarily commit the speaker to a literal statement of similarity.

The semantic interaction view, it seems to me, is equally defective. One of the assumptions behind the view that metaphorical meaning is a result of an interaction between an expression used metaphorically and other expressions used literally is that all metaphorical uses of expressions must occur in sentences containing literal uses of expressions, and that assumption seems to me plainly false. It is, incidentally, the assumption behind the terminology of many of the contemporary discussions of metaphor. We are told, for example, that every metaphorical sentence contains a "tenor" and a "vehicle" (Richards, 1936) or a "frame" and a "focus" (Black, 1962). But it is not the case that every metaphorical use of an expression is surrounded by literal uses of other expressions. Consider again our example 4: In uttering, "Sally is a block of ice", we referred to Sally using her proper name literally, but we need not have. Suppose, to use a mixed metaphor, we refer to Sally as "the bad news". We could then say, using a mixed metaphor

18. The bad news is a block of ice.

If you insist that the "is" is still literal, it is easy enough to construct examples of a dramatic change on Sally's part where we would be inclined, in another mixed metaphor, to say

19. The bad news congealed into a block of ice.

Mixed metaphors may be stylistically objectionable, but I cannot see that they are necessarily logically incoherent. Of course, most metaphors do occur in contexts of expressions used literally. It would be very hard to understand them if they did not. But it is not a logical necessity that every metaphorical use of an expression occurs surrounded by literal occurrences of other expressions and, indeed, many famous examples of metaphor are not. Thus Russell's example of a completely nonsensical sentence, "Quadrilaterality drinks procrastination", is often given a metaphorical interpretation as a description of any postwar four-power disarmament conference, but none of the words, so interpreted, has a literal occurrence; that is, for every word the speaker's utterance meaning differs from the literal word meaning.

However, the most serious objection to the semantic interaction view is not that it falsely presupposes that all metaphorical occurrences of words must be surrounded by literal occurrence of other words, but rather that, even where the metaphorical occurrence is within the context of literal occurrences, it is not in general the case that the metaphorical speaker's meaning is a result of any interaction among the elements of the sentence in any literal sense of "interaction". Consider again our example 4. In its metaphorical utterances, there is no question of any interaction between the meaning of the "principal subject" ("Sally") and the "subsidiary subject" ("block of ice"). "Sally" is a proper name; it does not have a meaning in quite the way in which "block of ice" has a meaning. Indeed, other expressions could have been used to produce the same metaphorical predication. Thus,

20. Miss Jones is a block of ice

or

21. That girl over there in the corner is a block of ice

could have been uttered with the same metaphorical utterance meaning.

I conclude that, as general theories, both the object comparison view and the semantic interaction view are inadequate. If we were to diagnose their failure in Fregean terms, we might say that the comparison view tries to explain metaphor as a relation between references, and the interaction view tries to explain it as a relation between senses and beliefs associated with references. The proponents of the interaction view see correctly that the mental processes and the semantic processes involved in producing and understanding metaphorical utterances cannot involve references themselves, but must be at the level of intentionality, that is, they must involve relations at the level of beliefs, meanings, associations, and so on. However, they then say incorrectly that the relations in question must be some unexplained, but metaphorically described, relations of "interaction"[3] between a literal frame and a metaphorical focus.

Two final mistakes I wish to note are not cases of saying something false about metaphors but of saying something true which fails to distinguish metaphor from literal utterance. Thus it is sometimes said that the notion of similarity plays a crucial role in the analysis of a metaphor, or that metaphorical utterances are dependent on the context for their interpretation. But, as we saw earlier, both of these features are true of literal utterances as well. An analysis of metaphor must show how similarity and context play a role in metaphor different from their role in literal utterance.

A FURTHER EXAMINATION OF THE COMPARISON THEORY

One way to work up to a theory of metaphor would be to examine the strengths and weaknesses of one of the existing theories. The obvious candidate for this role of stalking horse is a version of the comparison theory that goes back to Aristotle and can, indeed, probably be considered the commonsense view – the theory that says all metaphor is really literal simile with the "like" or "as" deleted and the respect of the similarity left unspecified. Thus, according to this view, the metaphorical utterance, "Man is a wolf", means "Man is like a wolf in certain unspecified ways"; the utterance, "You are my sunshine", means "You are like

---

[3] Even in Black's (1979) clarification of interaction in terms of "implication-complexes" there still does not seem to be any precise statement of the principles on which interaction works. And the actual example he gives, "Marriage is a zero-sum game", looks distressingly like a comparison metaphor: "Marriage is *like* a zero-sum game in that it is an adversary relationship between two parties in which one side can benefit only at the expense of the other." It is hard to see what the talk about interaction is supposed to add to this analysis.

sunshine to me in certain respects", and "Sally is a block of ice", means "Sally is like a block of ice in certain but so far unspecified ways".

The principles on which metaphors function, then, according to this theory are the same as those for literal statements of similarity together with the principle of ellipsis. We understand the metaphor as a shortened version of the literal simile.[4] Since literal simile requires no special extralinguistic knowledge for its comprehension, most of the knowledge necessary for the comprehension of metaphor is already contained in the speaker's and hearer's semantic competence, together with the general background knowledge of the world that makes literal meaning comprehensible.

We have already seen certain defects of this view, most notably that metaphorical statements cannot be equivalent in meaning to literal statements of similarity because the truth conditions of the two sorts of statements are frequently different. Furthermore, we must emphasize that even as a theory of metaphorical comprehension – as opposed to a theory of metaphorical meaning – it is important for the simile theory that the alleged underlying similes be literal statements of similarity. If the simile statements which are supposed to explain metaphor are themselves metaphorical or otherwise figurative, our explanation will be circular.

Still, treated as a theory of comprehension, there do seem to be a large number of cases where for the metaphorical utterance we can construct a simile sentence that does seem in some way to explain how its metaphorical meaning is comprehended. And, indeed, the fact that the specification of the values of R is left vague by the simile statement may, in fact, be an advantage of the theory, inasmuch as metaphorical utterances are often vague in precisely that way: it is not made *exactly* clear what the R is supposed to be when we say that "*S* is *P*" meaning metaphorically that "*S* is *R*". Thus, for

---

[4] By "literal simile", I mean literal statement of similarity. It is arguable that one should confine "simile" to nonliteral comparisons, but that is not the usage I follow here.

example, in analyzing Romeo's metaphorical statement, "Juliet is the sun", Cavell (1976, pp. 78–9) gives as part of its explanation that Romeo means that his day begins with Juliet. Now, apart from the special context of the play, that reading would never occur to me. I would look for other properties of the sun to fill in the values of R in the formula. Saying this is not objecting to either Shakespeare or Cavell, because the metaphor in question, like most metaphors, is open-ended in precisely that way.

Nonetheless, the simile theory, in spite of its attractiveness, has serious difficulties. First, the theory does more – or rather, less – than fail to tell us how to compute the value of R exactly: So far it fails to tell us how to compute it at all. That is, the theory still has almost no explanatory power, because the task of a theory of metaphor is to explain how the speaker and hearer are able to go from "*S* is *P*" to "*S* is *R*", and it does not explain that process to tell us that they go from "*S* is *P*" to "*S* is *R*" by first going through the stage "*S* is like *P* with respect to *R*" because we are not told how we are supposed to figure out which values to assign to R. Similarity is a vacuous predicate: any two things are similar in some respect or other. Saying that the metaphorical "*S* is *P*" implies the literal "*S* is like *P*" does not solve our problem. It only pushes it back a step. The problem of understanding literal similes with the respect of the similarity left unspecified is only a part of the problem of understanding metaphor. How are we supposed to know, for example, that the utterance, "Juliet is the sun", does not mean "Juliet is for the most part gaseous", or "Juliet is 90 million miles from the earth", both of which properties are salient and well-known features of the sun.

Yet another objection is this: It is crucial to the simile thesis that the simile be taken literally; yet there seem to be a great many metaphorical utterances where there is no relevant literal corresponding similarity between *S* and *P*. If we insist that there are always such similes, it looks as if we would have to interpret them metaphorically, and thus our account would be circular. Consider our example 4, "Sally is a block of ice". If we were to enumerate quite literally the various distinctive qualities of blocks of ice, none of them would be true of Sally. Even if we were to throw in the various beliefs that people have about blocks of ice, they still would not be literally true of Sally. There simply is no class of predicates, R, such that Sally is literally like a block of ice with respect to R where R is what we intended to predicate metaphorically of Sally when we said she was a block of ice. Being unemotional is not a feature of blocks of ice because blocks of ice are not in that line of business at all, and if one wants to insist that blocks of ice are literally unresponsive, then we need only point out that that feature is still insufficient to explain the metaphorical utterance meaning of 4, because in that sense bonfires are "unresponsive" as well, but

22. Sally is a bonfire

has a quite different metaphorical utterance meaning from 4. Furthermore, there are many similes that are not intended literally. For example, an utterance of "My love is like a red, red rose" does not mean that there is a class of literal predicates that are true both of my love and red, red roses and that express what the speaker was driving at when he said his love was like a red, red rose.

The defender of the simile thesis, however, need not give up so easily. He might say that many metaphors are also examples of other figures as well. Thus, "Sally is a block of ice" is not only an example of metaphor, but of hyperbole as well.[5] The metaphorical utterance meaning is indeed derived from the simile, "Sally is like a block of ice", but then both the metaphor and the simile are cases of *hyperbole*; they are exaggerations, and indeed, many metaphors are exaggerations. According to this reply, if we interpret both the metaphor and the simile hyperbolically, they are equivalent.

Furthermore, the defender of the simile thesis might add that it is not an objection to the simile account to say that some of the respects in which Sally is like a block of ice will be specified metaphorically, because for each of these met-

---

[5] Furthermore, it is at least arguable that "block of ice" functions metonymously in this example.

aphorical similes we can specify another underlying simile until eventually we reach the rock bottom of literal similes on which the whole edifice rests. Thus "Sally is a block of ice" means "Sally is like a block of ice", which means "She shares certain traits with a block of ice, in particular she is very cold". But since "cold" in "Sally is very cold" is also metaphorical, there must be an underlying similarity in which Sally's emotional state is like coldness, and when we finally specify these respects, the metaphor will be completely analyzed.

There are really two stages to this reply: First, it points out that other figures such as hyperbole sometimes combine with metaphor, and, secondly, it concedes that some of the similes that we can offer as translations of the metaphor are still metaphorical, but insists that some recursive procedure of analyzing metaphorical similes will eventually lead us to literal similes.

Is this reply really adequate? I think not. The trouble is that there do not seem to be any literal similarities between objects which are cold and people who are unemotional that would justify the view that when we say metaphorically that someone is cold what we mean is that he or she is unemotional. In what respects exactly are unemotional people like cold objects? Well, there are some things that one can say in answer to this, but they all leave us feeling somewhat dissatisfied.

We can say, for example, that when someone is physically cold it places severe restrictions on their emotions. But even if that is true, it is not what we meant by the metaphorical utterance. I think the only answer to the question, "What is the relation between cold things and unemotional people that would justify the use of 'cold' as a metaphor for lack of emotion?" is simply that as a matter of perceptions, sensibilities, and linguistic practices, people find the notion of coldness associated in their minds with lack of emotion. The notion of being cold just is associated with being unemotional.

There is some evidence, incidentally, that this metaphor works across several different cultures: It is not confined to

English speakers (cf. Asch, 1958). Moreover, it is even becoming, or has become, a dead metaphor. Some dictionaries (e.g. the *OED*) list lack of emotion as one of the meanings of "cold". Temperature metaphors for emotional and personal traits are in fact quite common and they are not derived from any literal underlying similarities. Thus we speak of a "heated argument", "a warm welcome", "a lukewarm friendship", and "sexual frigidity". Such metaphors are fatal for the simile thesis, unless the defenders can produce a literal *R* which *S* and *P* have in common, and which is sufficient to explain the precise metaphorical meaning which is conveyed.

Because this point is bound to be contested, it is well to emphasize exactly what is at stake. In claiming that there are not sufficient similarities to explain utterance meaning, I am making a negative existential claim, and thus not one which is demonstrable from an examination of a finite number of instances. The onus is rather on the similarity theorist to state the similarities and show how they exhaust utterance meaning. But it is not at all easy to see how he could do that in a way that would satisfy the constraints of his own theory.

Of course, one can think of lots of ways in which any *S* is like any *P*, e.g. ways in which Sally is like a block of ice, and one can think of lots of *F*s and *G*s such that Sally's being *F* is like a block of ice's being *G*. But that is not enough. Such similarities as one can name do not exhaust utterance meaning and if there are others that do, they are certainly not obvious.

But suppose with some ingenuity one could think up a similarity that would exhaust utterance meaning. The very fact that it takes so much ingenuity to think it up makes it unlikely that it is the underlying principle of the metaphorical interpretation, inasmuch as the metaphor is obvious: There is no difficulty for any native speaker to explain what it means. In "Sam is a pig", both utterance meaning and similarities are obvious, but in "Sally is a block of ice", only the utterance meaning is obvious. The simpler hypothesis, then, is that this metaphor, like several others I shall now discuss, functions on principles other than similarity.

Once we start looking for them, this class of metaphors turns out to be quite large. For example, the numerous spatial metaphors for temporal duration are not based on literal similarities. In "time flies", or "the hours crawled by", what is it that time does and the hours did which is literally like flying or crawling? We are tempted to say they went rapidly or slowly respectively, but of course "went rapidly" and "went slowly" are further spatial metaphors. Similarly, taste metaphors for personal traits are not based on properties in common. We speak of a "sweet disposition" or a "bitter person", without implying that the sweet disposition and the bitter person have literal traits in common with sweet and bitter tastes which exhaust the utterance meaning of the metaphorical utterance. Of course, sweet dispositions and sweet things are both pleasant, but much more is conveyed by the metaphor than mere pleasantness.

So deeply embedded in our whole mode of sensibility are certain metaphorical associations that we tend to think there *must* be a similarity, or even that the association itself is a form of similarity. Thus, we feel inclined to say that the passage of time *just is like* spatial movement, but when we say this we forget that "passage" is only yet another spatial metaphor for time and that the bald assertion of similarity, with no specification of the respect of similarity, is without content.

The most sophisticated version of the simile thesis I have seen is by George Miller (1979), and I shall digress briefly to consider some of its special features. Miller, like other simile theorists, believes that the meanings of metaphorical statements can be expressed as statements of similarity, but he offers a special kind of similarity statement (rather like one of Aristotle's formulations, by the way) as the form of "reconstruction" of metaphorical statements. According to Miller, metaphors of the form "S is P", where both S and P are noun phrases, are equivalent to sentences of the form

23. $(\exists F)\,(\exists G)\,(\mathrm{SIM}(F(S),\,G(P)))$.

Thus, for example, "Man is a wolf", according to Miller would be analyzed as

24. There is some property F and some property G such that man's being F is similar to a wolf's being G.

And when we have metaphors where a verb or predicate adjective F is used metaphorically in a sentence of the form "x is F" or "xFs", the analysis is of the form

25. $(\exists G)\,(\exists y)\,(SIM(G(x), F(y)))$.

Thus, for example, "The problem is thorny" would be analyzed as

26. There is some property G and some object y such that the problem's being G is similar to y's being thorny.

I believe this account has all the difficulties of the other simile theories – namely, it mistakenly supposes that the use of a metaphorical predicate commits the speaker to the existence of objects of which that predicate is literally true; it confuses the truth conditions of the metaphorical statement with the principles under which it is comprehended; it fails to tell us how to compute the values of the variables (Miller is aware of this problem, he calls it the problem of "interpretation" and sees it as different from the problem of "reconstruction"); and it is refuted by the fact that not all metaphors have literal statements of similarity underlying them. But it has some additional problems of its own. In my view, the most serious weakness of Miller's account is that according to it the semantic contents of most metaphorical utterances would have too many predicates, and, in fact, rather few metaphors really satisfy the formal structure he provides us with. Consider, for example, "Man is a wolf". On what I believe is the most plausible version of the simile thesis, it means something of the form

27. Man is like a wolf in certain respects R.

We could represent this as

28. SIM_R (man, wolf).

The hearer is required to compute only one set of predicates, the values for R. But according to Miller's account, the hearer is required to compute no less than three sets of predicates. Inasmuch as similarity is a vacuous predicate, we need to be told in which respect two things are similar for the statement that they are similar to have any informative content. His formalization of the above metaphorical utterance is

29. $(\exists F)\,(\exists G)\,(\text{SIM}(F(\text{man}), G(\text{wolf})))$.

In order to complete this formula in a way that would specify the respect of the similarity we would have to rewrite it as

30. $(\exists F)\,(\exists G)\,(\exists H)\,(\text{SIM}_H\,(F(\text{man}), G(\text{wolf})))$.

But both the reformulation 30, and Miller's original 29, contain too many predicate variables. When I say, "Man is a wolf", I am not saying that there are some *different* sets of properties that men have from those that wolves have, I am saying they have the *same* set of properties (at least on a sympathetic construal of the simile thesis, that is what I am saying). But according to Miller's account, I am saying that man has one set of properties F, wolves have a different set of properties G, and man's having F is similar to wolves having G with respect to some other properties H. I argue that this "reconstruction" is (a) counterintuitive, (b) unmotivated, and (c) assigns an impossible computing task to the speaker and hearer. What are these Fs, Gs and Hs supposed to be? and how is the hearer supposed to figure them out? It is not surprising that his treatment of the interpretation problem is very sketchy. Similar objections apply to his accounts of other syntactical forms of metaphorical utterances.

There is a class of metaphors, that I shall call "relational metaphors", for which something like his analysis might be more appropriate. Thus, if I say

8. The ship ploughed the sea

or

31. Washington is the father of his country,

these might be interpreted using something like his forms. We might treat 8 as equivalent to

32. There is some relation R which the ship has to the sea

and which is similar to the relation that ploughs have
to fields when they plough fields;

and 31 as

33. There is some relation R which Washington has to his
country and which is like the relation that fathers have
to their offspring.

And 32 and 33 are fairly easily formalized *à la* Miller.
However, even these analyses seem to me to concede too
much to his approach: 8 makes no reference either implicitly
or explicitly to fields and 31 makes no reference to offspring.
On the simplest and most plausible version of the simile
thesis 8 and 31 are equivalent to:

34. The ship does something to the sea which is like
ploughing

and

35. Washington stands in a relation to his country which
is like the relation of being a father.

And the hearer's task is simply to compute the intended
relations in the two cases. By my account, which I shall
develop in the next section, similarity does not in general
function as part of the truth conditions either in Miller's
manner or in the simpler version; rather, when it functions, it
functions as a strategy for interpretation. Thus, very crudely,
the way that similarity figures in the interpretation of 8 and 31
is given by

36. The ship does something to the sea (to figure out what
it is, find a relationship like ploughing)

and

37. Washington stands in a certain relationship to his
country (to figure out what it is, find a relationship like
that of being a father).

But the hearer does not have to compute any respects in
which these relations are similar, since that is not what is

being asserted. Rather, what is being asserted is that the ship is doing something to the sea and that Washington stands in a certain set of relations to his country, and the hearer is to figure out what it is that the ship does and what the relations are that Washington stands in by looking for relations similar to *ploughing* and *being a father of*.

To conclude this section: The problem of metaphor is either very difficult or very easy. If the simile theory were true, it would be very easy, because there would be no separate semantic category of metaphors – only a category of *elliptical utterances* where "like" or "as" had been deleted from the uttered sentence. But alas, the simile theory is not right, and the problem of metaphor remains very difficult. I hope our rather lengthy discussion of the simile theory has been illuminating in at least these respects. First, there are many metaphors in which there is no underlying literal similarity adequate to explain the metaphorical utterance meaning. Second, even where there is a correlated literal statement of similarity, the truth conditions, and hence the meaning of the metaphorical statement and the similarity statement, are not, in general, the same. Third, what we should salvage from the simile theory is a set of strategies for producing and understanding metaphorical utterances, using similarity. And fourth, even so construed, that is, construed as a theory of interpretation rather than of meaning, the simile theory does not tell us how to compute the respects of similarity or which similarities are metaphorically intended by the speaker.

THE PRINCIPLES OF METAPHORICAL INTERPRETATION

The time has now come to try to state the principles according to which metaphors are produced and understood. To reiterate, in its simplest form, the question we are trying to answer is, How is it possible for the speaker to say metaphorically "S is P" and mean "S is R", when P plainly does not mean R? Furthermore, How is it possible for the hearer who hears the utterance "S is P" to know that the

speaker means "*S* is *R*"? The short and uninformative
answer is that the utterance of *P* calls to mind the meaning
and, hence, truth conditions associated with *R*, in the special
ways that metaphorical utterances have of calling other
things to mind. But that answer remains uninformative until
we know what are the principles according to which the
utterance calls the metaphorical meaning to mind, and until
we can state these principles in a way which does not rely on
metaphorical expressions like "calls to mind". I believe that
there is no single principle on which metaphor works.

The question, "How do metaphors work?" is a bit like the
question, "How does one thing remind us of another thing?"
There is no single answer to either question, though
similarity obviously plays a major role in answering both.
Two important differences between them are that metaphors
are both restricted and systematic; restricted in the sense that
not every way that one thing can remind us of something else
will provide a basis for metaphor, and systematic in the sense
that metaphors must be communicable from speaker to
hearer in virtue of a shared system of principles.

Let us approach the problem from the hearer's point of
view. If we can figure out the principles according to which
hearers understand metaphorical utterances, we shall be a
long way toward understanding how it is possible for
speakers to make metaphorical utterances, because for
communication to be possible, speaker and hearer must share
a common set of principles. Suppose a hearer hears an
utterance such as, "Sally is a block of ice", or "Richard is a
gorilla", or "Bill is a barn door". What are the steps he must
go through in order to comprehend the metaphorical
meaning of such utterances? Obviously an answer to that
question need not specify a set of steps that he goes through
consciously; instead it must provide a rational reconstruction
of the inference patterns that underlie our ability to
understand such metaphors. Furthermore, not all metaphors
will be as simple as the cases we shall be discussing;
nonetheless, a model designed to account for the simple cases
should prove to be of more general application.

I believe that for the simple sorts of cases that we have been discussing, the hearer must go through at least three sets of steps. First, he must have some strategy for determining whether or not he has to seek a metaphorical interpretation of the utterance in the first place. Second, when he has decided to look for a metaphorical interpretation, he must have some set of strategies, or principles, for computing possible values of R, and third, he must have a set of strategies, or principles, for restricting the range of Rs – for deciding which Rs are likely to be the ones the speaker is asserting of *S*.

Suppose he hears the utterance, "Sam is a pig". He knows that that cannot be literally true, that the utterance, if he tries to take it literally, is radically defective. And, indeed, such defectiveness is a feature of nearly all of the examples that we have considered so far. The defects which cue the hearer may be obvious falsehood, semantic nonsense, violations of the rules of speech acts, or violations of conversational principles of communication. This suggests a strategy that underlies the first step:

Where the utterance is defective if taken literally, look for an utterance meaning that differs from sentence meaning.

This is not the only strategy on which a hearer can tell that an utterance probably has a metaphorical meaning, but it is by far the most common. (It is also common to the interpretation of poetry. If I hear a figure on a Grecian Urn being addressed as a "still unravish'd bride of quietness", I know I had better look for alternative meanings.) But it is certainly not a necessary condition of a metaphorical utterance that it be in any way defective if construed literally. Disraeli might have said metaphorically

5. (MET) I have climbed to the top of the greasy pole,

though he had in fact climbed to the top of a greasy pole. There are various other clues that we employ to spot metaphorical utterances. For example, when reading Romantic poets, we are on the lookout for metaphors, and some people we know are simply more prone to metaphorical utterances than others.

Once our hearer has established that he is to look for an

alternative meaning, he has a number of principles by which he can compute possible values of R. I will give a list of these shortly, but one of them is this.

When you hear "S is P", to find possible values of R look for ways in which S might be like P, and to fill in the respect in which S might be like P, look for salient, well known, and distinctive features of P things.

In this case, the hearer might invoke his factual knowledge to come up with such features as that pigs are fat, gluttonous, slovenly, filthy, and so on. This indefinite range of features provides possible values of R. However, lots of other features of pigs are equally distinctive and well known, for example, pigs have a distinctive shape and distinctive bristles. So, in order to understand the utterance, the hearer needs to go through the third step where he restricts the range of possible Rs. Here again the hearer may employ various strategies for doing that but the one that is most commonly used is this.

Go back to the S term and see which of the many candidates for the values of R are likely or even possible properties of S.

Thus, if the hearer is told, "Sam's car is a pig", he will interpret that metaphor differently from the utterance, "Sam is a pig". The former, he might take to mean that Sam's car consumes gas the way pigs consume food, or that Sam's car is shaped like a pig. Though, in one sense, the metaphor is the same in the two cases, in each case it is restricted by the *S* term in a different way. The hearer has to use his knowledge of *S* things and *P* things to know which of the possible values of R are plausible candidates for metaphorical predication.

Now, much of the dispute between the interaction theories and the object comparison theories derives from the fact that they can be construed as answers to different questions. The object comparison theories are best construed as attempts to answer the question of stage two: "How do we compute the possible values of R?" The interaction theories are best construed as answers to the question of stage three: "Given a range of possible values of R, how does the relationship between the S term and the P term restrict that range?" I think it is misleading to describe these relations as "interactions", but it seems correct to suppose that the S term must play a role in metaphors of the sort we have been considering. In order to show that the interaction theory was also an answer to the question of stage two, we would have to show that there are values of R that are specifiable, given S and P together, that are not specifiable given P alone; one would have to show that S does not *restrict* the range of Rs but in fact, creates new Rs. I do not believe that can be shown, but I shall mention some possibilities later.

I said that there were a variety of principles for computing R, given P – that is, a variety of principles according to which the utterance of P can call to mind the meaning R in ways that are peculiar to metaphor. I am sure I do not know all of the principles that do this, but here are several (not necessarily independent) for a start.

Principle 1. Things which are P are by definition R. Usually, if the metaphor works, R will be one of the salient defining characteristics of P. Thus, for example,

38. (MET) Sam is a giant

will be taken to mean

38. (PAR) Sam is big,

because giants are by definition big. That is what is special about them.

Principle 2. Things which are P are contingently R. Again, if the metaphor works, the property R should be a salient or well known property of P things.

39. (MET) Sam is a pig

will be taken to mean

39. (PAR) Sam is filthy, gluttonous, and sloppy, etc.

Both principles 1 and 2 correlate metaphorical utterances with literal similes, "Sam is like a giant", "Sam is like a pig", and so on. Notice in connection with this principle and the next that small variations in the P term can create big differences in the R terms. Consider the differences between "Sam is a pig", "Sam is a hog", and "Sam is a swine".

Principle 3. Things which are P are often said or believed to be R, even though both speaker and hearer may know that R is false of P. Thus,

    7. (MET) Richard is a gorilla

can be uttered to mean

    7. (PAR) Richard is mean, nasty, prone to violence, and so on,

even though both speaker and hearer know that in fact gorillas are shy, timid, and sensitive creatures, but generations of gorilla mythology have set up associations that will enable the metaphor to work even though both speaker and hearer know these beliefs to be false.

Principle 4. Things which are P are not R, nor are they like R things, nor are they believed to be R; nonetheless it is a fact about our sensibility, whether culturally or naturally determined, that we just do perceive a connection, so that P is associated in our minds with R properties. Thus,

    4. (MET) Sally is a block of ice
   40. (MET) I am in a black mood
   41. (MET) Mary is sweet
   42. (MET) John is bitter

43. (MET) The hours $\left\{ \begin{array}{l} \text{crept} \\ \text{crawled} \\ \text{dragged} \\ \text{sped} \\ \text{whizzed} \end{array} \right\}$ by as we waited

    for the plane

are sentences that could be uttered to mean metaphorically that: Sally is unemotional; I am angry and depressed; Mary is gentle, kind, pleasant, and so on; John is resentful; and the hours seemed (of varying degrees of duration) as we waited for the plane; even though there are no literal similarities on which these metaphors are based. Notice that the associations tend to be scalar: degrees of temperature with ranges of emotion, degrees of speed with temporal duration, and so forth.

Principle 5. P things are not like R things, and are not believed to be like R things; nonetheless the condition of being P is like the condition of being R. Thus, I might say to someone who has just received a huge promotion

44. You have become an aristocrat,

meaning not that he has personally become *like* an aristocrat, but that his new status or condition is like that of being an aristocrat.

Principle 6. There are cases where P and R are the same or similar in meaning, but where one, usually P, is restricted in its application, and does not literally apply to S. Thus, "addled" is only said literally of eggs, but we can metaphorically say

45. This soufflé is addled
46. That parliament was addled

and

47. His brain is addled.

Principle 7. This is not a separate principle but a way of applying principles 1–6 to simple cases which are not of the form "S is P" but relational metaphors, and metaphors of other syntactical forms such as those involving verbs and predicate adjectives. Consider such relational metaphors as

48. Sam devours books
 8. The ship ploughs the sea
31. Washington was the father of his country.

In each case, we have a literal utterance of two noun phrases surrounding a metaphorical utterance of a relational term (it can be a transitive verb, as in 48 and 8 but it need not be, as in 31). The hearer's task is not to go from "*S* is *P*" to "*S* is *R*" but to go from "*S* *P*-relation *S'*" to "*S* *R*-relation *S'*" and the latter task is formally rather different from the former because, for example, our similarity principles in the former case will enable him to find a property that *S* and *P* things have in common, namely, *R*. But in the latter, he cannot find a relation in common; instead he has to find a relation *R* which is different from relation *P* but similar to it in some respect. So, as applied to these cases, principle 1, for example, would read

P-relations are by definition R-relations.

For example, *ploughing* is by definition partly a matter of moving a substance to either side of a pointed object while the object moves forward; and though this definitional similarity between the *P*-relation and the *R*-relation would provide the principle that enables the hearer to infer the R-relation, the respect of similarity does not exhaust the content of the R-relation, as the similarity exhausts the content of the R term in the simplest of the "*S* is *P*" cases. In these cases, the hearer's job is to find a relation (or property) that is similar to, or otherwise associated with, the relation or property literally expressed by the metaphorical expression *P*; and the principles function to enable him to select that relation or property by giving him a respect in which the *P*-relation and the R-relation might be similar or otherwise associated.

Principle 8. According to my account of metaphor, it becomes a matter of terminology whether we want to construe metonymy and synecdoche as special cases of metaphor or as independent tropes. When one says, "*S* is *P*", and means that "*S* is *R*", *P* and *R* may be associated by such relations as the part–whole relation, the container–contained relation, or even the clothing and wearer relation. In each case, as in metaphor proper, the semantic content of the *P* term conveys the semantic content of the *R* term by some principle of association. Since the principles of metaphor are rather various anyway, I am inclined to treat metonymy and synecdoche as special cases of metaphor and add their principles to my list of metaphorical principles. I can, for example, refer to the British monarch as "the Crown", and the executive branch of the US government as "the White House" by exploiting systematic principles of association. However, as I said, the claim that these are special cases of metaphor seems to me purely a matter of terminology, and if purists insist that the principles of metaphor be kept separate from those of metonymy and synecdoche, I can have no nontaxonomical objections.

In addition to these eight principles, one might wonder if there is a ninth one. Are there cases where an association between P and R that did not previously exist can be created by the juxtaposition of S and P in the original sentence? This, I take it, is the thesis of the interaction theorists. However, I have never seen any convincing examples, nor any even halfway clear account, of what "interaction" is supposed to mean. Let us try to construct some examples. Consider the differences between

49. Sam's voice is $\left\{ \begin{array}{l} \text{mud} \\ \text{gravel} \\ \text{sandpaper} \end{array} \right\}$

and

50. Kant's second argument for the transcendental deduction is so much $\left\{ \begin{array}{l} \text{mud} \\ \text{gravel} \\ \text{sandpaper} \end{array} \right\}$.

The second set clearly gives us different metaphorical meanings – different values for R – than the first trio, and one might argue that this is due not to the fact that the different S terms restrict the range of possible Rs generated by the P terms, but to the fact that the different combinations of S and P create new Rs. But that explanation seems implausible. The more plausible explanation is this. One has a set of associations with the P terms, "mud", "gravel", and "sandpaper". The principles of these associations are those of principles 1–7. The different S terms restrict the values of R differently, because different Rs can be true of voices than can be true of arguments for transcendental deductions. Where is the interaction?

Since this section contains my account of metaphorical predication, it may be well to summarize its main points. Given that a speaker and a hearer have shared linguistic and factual knowledge sufficient to enable them to communicate literal utterances, the following strategies and principles are individually necessary and collectively sufficient to enable speaker and hearer to form and comprehend utterances of the form "S is P", where the speaker means metaphorically that S is R (where $P \neq R$).

First, there must be some shared strategies on the basis of which the hearer can recognize that the utterance is not intended literally. The most common, but not the only strategy, is based on the fact that the utterance is obviously defective if taken literally.

Second, there must be some shared principles that associate the P term (whether the meaning, the truth conditions, or the denotation if there is any) with a set of possible values of R. The heart of the problem of metaphor is to state these principles. I have tried to state several of them, but I feel confident that there must be more.

Third, there must be some shared strategies that enable the speaker and the hearer, given their knowledge of the S term (whether the meaning of the expression, or the nature of the referent, or both), to restrict the range of possible values of R to the actual value of R. The basic principle of this step is that only those possible values of R which determine possible properties of S can be actual values of R.

METAPHOR, IRONY, AND INDIRECT SPEECH ACTS

To conclude, I wish to compare briefly the principles on which metaphor works with those on which irony and indirect speech acts work. Consider first a case of irony. Suppose you have just broken a priceless K'ang Hsi vase and

I say ironically, "That was a brilliant thing to do." Here, as in metaphor, the speaker's meaning and sentence meaning are different. What are the principles by which the hearer is able to infer that the speaker meant, "That was a stupid thing to do", when what he heard was the sentence, "That was a brilliant thing to do"? Stated very crudely, the mechanism by which irony works is that the utterance, if taken literally, is obviously inappropriate to the situation. Since it is grossly inappropriate, the hearer is compelled to reinterpret it in such a way as to render it appropriate, and the most natural way to interpret it is as meaning the *opposite* of its literal form.

I am not suggesting that this is by any means the whole story about irony. Cultures and subcultures vary enormously in the extent and degree of the linguistic and extralinguistic cues provided for ironical utterances. In English, in fact, there are certain characteristic intonational contours that go with ironical utterances. However, it is important to see that irony, like metaphor, does not require any conventions, extralinguistic or otherwise. The principles of conversation and the general rules for performing speech acts are sufficient to provide the basic principles of irony.

Now consider a case of an indirect speech act. Suppose that in the usual dinner-table situation, I say to you, "Can you pass the salt?" In this situation you will normally take that as meaning, "Please pass the salt." That is, you will take the question about your ability as a request to perform an action. What are the principles on which this inference works? There is a radical difference between indirect speech acts, on the one hand, and irony and metaphor, on the other. In the indirect speech act, the speaker means what he says. However, in addition, he means something more. Sentence meaning is part of utterance meaning, but it does not exhaust utterance meaning. In a very simplified form (for a more detailed account, see Searle, 1975b, chapter 2 of this volume), the principles on which the inference works in this case are: First, the hearer must have some device for recognizing that the utterance might be an indirect speech act. This requirement is satisfied by the fact that in the context, a question about the hearer's ability lacks any conversational point. The hearer, therefore, is led to seek an alternative meaning. Second, since the hearer knows the rules of speech acts, he knows that the ability to pass the salt is a preparatory condition on the speech act of requesting him to do so. Therefore, he is able to infer that the question about his ability is likely to be a polite request to perform the act. The differences and similarities between literal utterances, metaphorical utterances, ironical utterances, and indirect speech acts are illustrated in Figure 2.

The question of whether all metaphorical utterances can be given a literal paraphrase is one that must have a trivial answer. Interpreted one way, the answer is trivially yes; interpreted another way, it is trivially no. If we interpret the question as, "Is it possible to find or to invent an expression that will exactly express the intended metaphorical meaning R, in the sense of the truth conditions of R, for any metaphorical utterance of 'S is P', where what is meant is that S is R?" the answer to that question must surely be yes. It follows trivially from the Principle of Expressibility (see Searle, 1969) that any meaning whatever can be given an exact expression in the language.

If the question is interpreted as meaning, "Does every existing language provide us exact devices for expressing literally whatever we wish to express in any given metaphor?" then the answer is obviously no. It is often the case that we use metaphor precisely because there is no literal expression that expresses exactly what we mean. Furthermore, in metaphorical utterances, we do more than just state that S is R; as Figure 2 shows, we state that S is R by way of going through the meaning of "S is P". It is in this sense that we feel that metaphors somehow are intrinsically not paraphrasable. They are not paraphrasable, because without using the metaphorical expression we will not reproduce the semantic content which occurred in the hearer's comprehension of the utterance.

The best we can do in the paraphrase is reproduce the truth conditions of the metaphorical utterance, but the metaphorical utterance does more than just convey its truth conditions. It conveys its truth conditions by way of another semantic

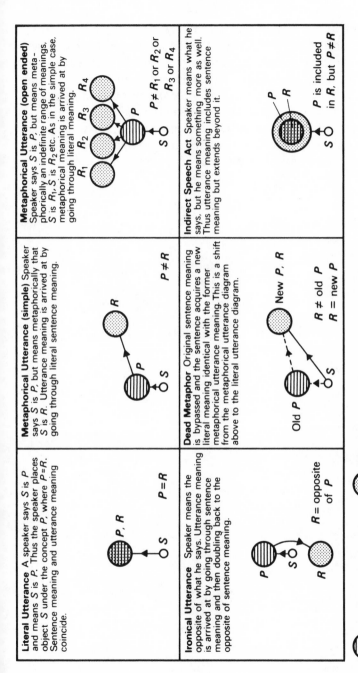

Literal Utterance A speaker says S is P and means S is P. Thus the speaker places object S under the concept P, where $P=R$. Sentence meaning and utterance meaning coincide.

P, R

S

$P = R$

Metaphorical Utterance (simple) Speaker says S is P, but means metaphorically that S is R. Utterance meaning is arrived at by going through literal sentence meaning.

R

P

S

$P \neq R$

Metaphorical Utterance (open ended) Speaker says S is P, but means metaphorically an indefinite range of meanings. S is R_1, S is R_2 etc. As in the simple case, metaphorical meaning is arrived at by going through literal meaning.

R_1 R_2 R_3 R_4

P

S

$P \neq R_1$ or R_2 or R_3 or R_4

Ironical Utterance Speaker means the opposite of what he says. Utterance meaning is arrived at by going through sentence meaning and then doubling back to the opposite of sentence meaning.

P

R

S

$R =$ opposite of P

Dead Metaphor Original sentence meaning is bypassed and the sentence acquires a new literal meaning identical with the former metaphorical utterance meaning. This is a shift from the metaphorical utterance diagram above to the literal utterance diagram.

Old P

New P, R

S

$R \neq$ old P
$R =$ new P

Indirect Speech Act Speaker means what he says, but he means something more as well. Thus utterance meaning includes sentence meaning but extends beyond it.

P
R

S

P is included in R, but $P \neq R$

● Sentence meaning, P ◐ Utterance meaning, R ○ Object, S

Fig. 2. A graphic comparison of the relations between sentence meaning and utterance meaning, where the sentence meaning is "S is P" and the utterance meaning is "S is R", that is, where the speaker utters a sentence that means literally that the object S falls under the concept P, but where the speaker means by his utterance that the object S falls under the concept R.

115

content, whose truth conditions are not part of the truth conditions of the utterance. The expressive power that we feel is part of good metaphors is largely a matter of two features. The hearer has to figure out what the speaker means – he has to contribute more to the communication than just passive uptake – and he has to do that by going through another and related semantic content from the one which is communicated. And that, I take it, is what Dr. Johnson meant when he said metaphor gives us two ideas for one.

Chapter 5

LITERAL MEANING

I

Most philosophers and linguists accept a certain conception of the notion of the literal meaning of words and sentences and the relation between literal meaning and other semantic notions such as ambiguity, metaphor, and truth. In this chapter I want to challenge one aspect of this received opinion, the view that for every sentence the literal meaning of the sentence can be construed as the meaning it has independently of any context whatever. I shall argue that in general the notion of the literal meaning of a sentence only has application relative to a set of contextual or background assumptions and finally I shall examine some of the implications of this alternative view. The view I shall be attacking is sometimes expressed by saying that the literal meaning of a sentence is the meaning that it has in the "zero context" or the "null context". I shall argue that for a large class of sentences there is no such thing as the zero or null context for the interpretation of sentences, and that as far as our semantic competence is concerned we understand the meaning of such sentences only against a set of background assumptions about the contexts in which the sentence could be appropriately uttered.

I begin by stating what I take to be the received opinion as a set of propositions:

Sentences have literal meanings. The literal meaning of a sentence is entirely determined by the meanings of its component words (or morphemes) and the syntactical rules according to which these elements are combined. A sentence may have more than one literal meaning (ambiguity) or its literal meaning may be defective or uninterpretable (nonsense).

The literal meaning of a sentence needs to be sharply

distinguished from what a speaker means by the sentence when he utters it to perform a speech act, for the speaker's utterance meaning may depart from the literal sentence meaning in a variety of ways. For example, in uttering a sentence a speaker may mean something different from what the sentence means, as in the case of metaphor; or he may even mean the opposite of what the sentence means, as in the case of irony; or he may mean what the sentence means but mean something more as well, as in the case of conversational implications and indirect speech acts. In the limiting case what the sentence means and what the speaker means may be exactly the same; for example, the speaker might in a certain context utter the sentence "The cat is on the mat" and mean exactly and literally that the cat is on the mat. Strictly speaking, the expression "literal" in the phrase "literal meaning of the sentence" is pleonastic since all these other sorts of meaning – ironical meaning, metaphorical meaning, indirect speech acts and conversation implications – are not properties of sentences at all, but rather of speakers, utterances of sentences.

For sentences in the indicative, the meaning of the sentence determines a set of truth conditions; that is, it determines a set of conditions such that the literal utterance of the sentence to make a statement will be the making of a true statement if and only if those conditions are satisfied. According to some accounts, to know the meaning of such a sentence is just to know its truth conditions. Sometimes the meaning of a sentence is such that its truth conditions will vary systematically with the contexts of its literal utterance. Thus the sentence "I am hungry" might be uttered by one person on one occasion to make a true statement and yet be uttered by another person, or by the same person on another occasion, to make a false statement. Such "indexical" or "token reflexive" sentences differ from sentences such as "Snow is white" whose truth conditions do not vary with the context of utterance. It is important to notice however that the notion of the meaning of a sentence is absolutely context free. Even in the case of indexical sentences the meaning does not change from context to context; rather the constant meaning is such that it determines a set of truth conditions only relative to a context of utterance. The literal meaning of the sentence is the meaning it has independently of any context whatever; and, diachronic changes apart, it keeps that meaning in any context in which it is uttered.

Something like the picture sketched above provides a set of assumptions behind recent discussions in "semantics" and "pragmatics" that is so pervasive as hardly to constitute a theory at all; it is rather the framework within which any theory must be stated and validated. True, there have been skeptical doubts about various aspects of it. Some philosophers have argued that this notion of meaning is insufficiently empirical and should be replaced by some more behavioristic surrogates stated in terms of the stimulus and response patterns of speakers and hearers. Some have argued that the picture leads to an unwarranted hypostatization of meanings as separate entities. I think both of these objections are invalid, but I will not argue the points here. Furthermore there are some variations on this received opinion which contain fairly serious mistakes, and I will mention one such if only to get it out of the way at the beginning. Some philosophers and linguists mistakenly suppose that the distinction between sentence and utterance is the same as the distinction between type and token, and that utterances just are identical with sentence tokens. They then suppose that because utterance meaning can differ from sentence meaning that somehow sentence tokens acquire "different meanings in context" from the meaning of sentence types, which are context free. I believe that both aspects of this view are mistaken. That is, it is a category mistake to suppose that an utterance of a token and a token are identical and it is a mistake (derived from the previous one) to suppose that where utterance meaning differs from sentence meaning, the token acquires a different meaning from the type. If an argument is needed to show that these are mistakes it should be sufficient to point out that an utterance could not be identical with a token, because the same utterance can involve many tokens, as when one publishes one's utterances in printed form, and the same token can be used in the making of several utterances, as for example when one holds up the same "STOP" sign on several occasions. Every utterance does indeed involve the production or use of a token, but the utterance is not identical with the token, and where utterance meaning differs from sentence meaning, the token does not change its meaning. Barring diachronic changes, special codes, and the like, the meaning of the token is always the same as the meaning of the type. Sentence meaning, type or token, needs to be distinguished from the speaker's utterance meaning, and the sentence–utterance distinction is not the same as the type–token distinction.

Ignoring then the skeptical doubts about meaning that have been expressed about the received opinion, and setting aside those versions of it that contain definite mistakes, I shall argue in what follows that while the received opinion is for the most part correct (in particular it is correct in emphasizing the distinction between sentence meaning and utterance meaning), it errs in presenting the notion of the literal meaning of the sentence as a context free notion. Rather, I shall argue that for a large number of cases the notion of the literal meaning of a sentence only has application relative to a set of background assumptions, and furthermore these background assumptions are not all and could not all be realized in the semantic structure of the sentence in the way that presuppositions and indexically dependent elements of the sentence's truth conditions are realized in the semantic structure of the sentence.

My strategy in constructing the argument will be to consider sentences which appear to be favorable cases for the view that literal meaning is context free and then show that in each case the application of the notion of the literal meaning of the sentence is always relative to a set of contextual assumptions. Consider the sentence "The cat is on the mat." If any sentence has a clear literal meaning independent of any context this old philosophical chestnut ought to be it. To be sure, it contains indexical elements. In understanding an utterance of the sentence to make a statement we need to know which cat and which mat are being referred to and at what time and place the cat is being said to be on the mat. But these context dependent features of presupposition and indexicality are already realized in the semantic elements of the sentence, and if they are unclear in any particular utterance we could always make them more explicit by adding more indexical elements to the sentence – this cat right here is now on this mat right here – or we could eliminate the explicitly indexical features and substitute descriptions and time and space coordinates – the cat which has such and such features is on the mat with so and so features at such and such time and place. In addition to its indexical features the sentence carries a constant and unvarying descriptive meaning which the indexical elements serve to nail down to specific contexts in specific utterances. This unvarying descriptive content determines the truth conditions of the sentence, which the indexical elements relate to specific contexts of utterance. We might, with apologies for poor draftsmanship, represent this descriptive element as follows (see Figure 3).

Fig. 3

When things are like that, we feel inclined to say, the cat is on the mat; otherwise not. And that is what the sentence says – it says things in the cat and mat line of business are in the relation depicted. Of course, we might concede, the sentence is not as determinate as the picture, for the cat might be sitting or standing on the mat or facing the other way and still the truth conditions of the sentence would be satisfied; and we might also concede that there is the problem of vagueness. If the cat was half on and half off the mat we might not know what to say, but such concessions raise no difficulty with our notion of context independent literal meaning.

But now suppose that the cat and the mat are in exactly the relations depicted only they are both floating freely in outer space, perhaps outside the Milky Way galaxy altogether. In such a situation the scene would be just as well depicted if we turned the paper on edge or upside down since there is no gravitational field relative to which one is above the other. Is the cat still on the mat? And was the earth's gravitational field one of the things depicted in our drawing?

What I think it is correct to say as a first approximation in answer to these questions is that the notion of the literal meaning of the sentence "The cat is on the mat" does not have a clear application, unless we make some further assumptions, in the case of cats and mats floating freely in outer space; and though our picture did not depict the earth's gravitational field, it, like the sentence, only has an application relative to a set of background assumptions.

Well, it might be said in response to this, if these are really assumptions behind the notion of the literal meaning of the sentence, why not make them perfectly clear as further truth conditions of the sentence? They could be treated as further Strawsonian presuppositions, or if we did not want to treat them as truth conditions, they could be stage directions for the applicability of the sentence. That is, just as, according to some philosophers, "is bald" in the sentence "The king of France is bald" only has application if there is a king of France, so we might say the descriptive meaning of the sentence "The cat is on the mat" only has application at or near the surface of the earth or in some other similar gravitational field. But that, like any other presupposition, can be made explicit as part of the meaning of the sentence. What the sentence really means is expressed by: "(At or near the surface of the earth or some similar gravitational field) the cat is on the mat." Or alternatively we could treat this condition as a further stage direction for the application of the sentence, but still the stage directions would be a part of the literal meaning, at least in the sense that they would be made completely explicit in the semantic analysis of the sentence. On this account the sentence is rendered: "The cat is on the mat (this sentence only applies at or near the surface of the earth or in some similar gravitational field)." But these answers to our difficulty won't do, for at least two reasons. First, it is not always the case that the literal application of the sentence requires a gravitational field. That is, it is easy to construct examples where it would be quite literally true to say that the cat is on the mat, even though there is no gravitational field. For example, as we are strapped in the seats of our space ship in outer space we see a series of cat–mat pairs floating past our window. Oddly, they come in only two attitudes. From our point of view they are either as depicted in Figure 3, or as would be depicted if Figure 3 were upside down. "Which is it now?", I ask. "The cat is on the mat", you answer. Have you not said exactly and literally what you meant?

But secondly, even if we got all these assumptions about gravitational fields somehow represented as part of the semantic content of the sentence, we would still be left with an indefinite number of other contextual assumptions that we would have to deal with. Consider the following example. Suppose the cat and the mat are in the spatial relations depicted in Figure 3, at the surface of the earth, but that each, cat and mat, are suspended on an intricate series of invisible wires so that the cat, though slightly in contact with the mat, exerts no pressure on it. Is the cat still on the mat? Once again it seems to me that the question does not have a clear answer, and that is just another way of saying that the meaning of the sentence "The cat is on the mat" does not have a clear application in the context as so far specified and hence it does not yet determine a clear set of truth conditions. And once again, it seems to me we can easily fill in the context to give the sentence a clear application. Suppose the cat and the mat are part of a stage set. The wires are there to facilitate rapid movement of the props, as the cat has to be moved from chair to mat to table. "Where is it now?" the director shouts from backstage; "The cat is on the mat" shouts his assistant. Does he not say exactly and literally what he means? Further examples of the contextual dependence of the applicability of the literal meaning of this sentence are easy to generate. Suppose that the mat is as stiff as a board and is stuck into the floor at an angle. Suppose the cat is drugged into a stupor and is placed relative to the mat in the following attitude.

Fig. 4

Does this situation satisfy the truth conditions of "The cat is on the mat?" Again, I feel inclined to say that so far the question does not have a clear answer, and that relative to one set of additional assumptions the situation does satisfy the truth conditions of the sentence, relative to another set it does not; but this variation has nothing to do with vagueness, indexicality, presupposition, ambiguity, or any of the other stocks in trade of contemporary "semantic" and "pragmatic" theory, as these notions are traditionally conceived. Suppose the cat's owner is in the next room, while I unbeknownst to him have drugged his cat and stiffened his mat with my special stiffening solution. "Where is the cat?" asks the owner from his position next door. "The cat is on the mat", I answer. Have I told the truth? My inclination is to say that my answer is misleading at best and probably should be described as an ingenious lie, since I know that that is not what the owner understands when he hears and gives a literal interpretation to the utterance of the sentence, "The cat is on the mat." But now consider a different variation of the same example. The mat is in its stiff angled position, as in Figure 4, and it is part of a row of objects similarly sticking up at odd angles – a board, a fence post, an iron rod, etc. These facts are known to both speaker and hearer. The cat jumps from one of these objects to another. It is pretty obvious what the correct answer to the question, "Where is the cat?" should be when the cat is in the attitude depicted in Figure 4: The cat is on the mat.

These examples are designed to cast doubt on the following thesis: Every unambiguous sentence,[1] such as "The cat is on the mat" has a literal meaning which is absolutely context free and which determines for every context whether or not an utterance of that sentence in that context is literally true or false.

The examples are further designed to support the following alternative hypothesis: For a large class of unambiguous sentences such as "The cat is on the mat", the notion of the literal meaning of the sentence only has application relative to a set of background assumptions. The truth conditions of the sentence will vary with variations in these background assumptions; and given the absence or presence of some background assumptions the sentence does not have determinate truth conditions. These variations have nothing to do with indexicality, change of meaning, ambiguity, conversational implication, vagueness or pre-supposition as these notions are standardly discussed in the philosophical and linguistic literature.

Perhaps the thesis that literal meaning is absolutely context free could be replaced by a weaker thesis: while there may indeed be a large class of sentences whose literal meaning only determines a set of truth conditions relative to a set of background assumptions, still (it might be argued) for each sentence in this class we can specify these assumptions in such a way that they will be constant for every literal occurrence of the sentence.

But our examples have already cast doubt even on this weaker thesis; for the truth conditions of the sentence "The cat is on the mat" are satisfied in each of our "abnormal" contexts provided that the abnormal context is supplemented with some other assumptions. And thus, there is no constant set of assumptions that determine the applicability of the notion of literal meaning, rather the sentence may determine

---

[1] One can of course locate ambiguities even in this sentence; e.g., "cat" is sometimes used as a slang expression for caterpillar tractors. But such ambiguities are irrelevant to our present discussion.

different truth conditions relative to different assumptions in ways that have nothing to do with ambiguity, indexical dependence on context, presupposition failure, vagueness or change of meaning as these notions are traditionally conceived. Furthermore, our examples suggest that the assumptions are not specifiable as part of the semantic content of the sentence, or as presuppositions of the applicability of that semantic content, for at least two reasons. First, they are not fixed and definite in number and content; we would never know when to stop in our specifications. And second, each specification of an assumption tends to bring in other assumptions, those that determine the applicability of the literal meaning of the sentence used in the specification. It is important to note, however, that so far my examples only challenge the idea that there is a sentence by sentence specification of the background assumptions as part of the semantic analysis of each sentence; I have not so far addressed the question whether it might be possible to give a specification of all the assumptions against which speakers understand and apply the literal meanings of sentences.

Notice that we used only very limited resources in constructing the examples. We concentrated only on the contextual dependence of the word "on" as it occurs in the sentence. If we went to work on "cat" or "mat" we could find much more radical forms of contextual dependence. Second, we imagined no changes in the laws of nature. Again, given freedom to mess around with the laws of nature, I believe we could get still more radical breakdowns in the view that the application of the literal meaning of sentences is absolutely context independent.

II

Corresponding to the notion of the truth conditions of an indicative sentence is the notion of the obedience conditions of an imperative sentence or the fulfillment conditions of an optative sentence, and many of these same points will emerge if we consider sentences in the imperative and other moods.

Suppose I go into a restaurant determined to say exactly and literally what I mean, that is determined to utter imperative sentences that give exact expression to my desires. I start by saying: "Give me a hamburger, medium rare, with ketchup and mustard, but easy on the relish." I will remark first of all that a prodigious amount of background information has already been invoked even by the example as so far described – entire institutions of restaurants and money and of exchanging prepared foods for money, for a start; and it is hard to see how the sentence could have quite the same obedience conditions if these institutions did not exist, or if the same sentence were uttered in a radically different context, if for example the sentence were uttered by a priest as part of a prayer or tacked onto the end of his inaugural swearing in by an incoming President of the US. Still, one might argue, the sense of "give" in which it initiates commercial transactions is in part defined by these systems of constitutive rules. So this much of contextual dependence is in part realized in the semantic structure of the sentence. But even if one conceded that – and it is not clear that one should – there are all sorts of other assumptions on which the application of the sentence rests and which are not even remotely close to being realized in the semantic structure of the sentence. Suppose for example that the hamburger is brought to me encased in a cubic yard of solid lucite plastic so rigid that it takes a jack hammer to bust it open,[2] or suppose the hamburger is a mile wide and is "delivered" to me by smashing down the wall of the restaurant and sliding the edge of it in. Has my order "Give me a hamburger, medium rare, with ketchup and mustard, but easy on the relish" been fulfilled or obeyed in these cases? My inclination is to say no, it has not been fulfilled or obeyed because that is not what I meant in my literal utterance of the sentence (though again it is easy to imagine variations in our background assumptions where we would say that the order has been obeyed). But the fact that the order has not been obeyed – that is, that the

---

[2] This example was originally suggested to me by H. Dreyfus in a discussion of another issue.

obedience conditions of the sentence are not satisfied relative to that context – does not show that I failed to say exactly and literally what I meant, that what I should have said is "Give me a hamburger, medium rare, with ketchup and mustard, but easy on the relish; and don't encase it in plastic and no mile wide hamburgers, please." If we say that, then it will become impossible ever to say what we mean because there will always be further possible breakdowns in our background assumptions which would lead us to say that the obedience conditions of the sentence were not satisfied in a given context. Rather it seems to me what we should say in such cases is that I did say exactly and literally what I meant but that the literal meaning of my sentence, and hence of my literal utterance, only has application relative to a set of background assumptions which are not and for the most part could not be realized in the semantic structure of the sentence. And there are, in these cases as in the indicative cases, two reasons why these extra assumptions could not all be realized in the semantic structure of the sentence, first they are indefinite in number, and second, whenever one is given a literal statement of these assumptions, the statement relies on other assumptions for its intelligibility.

Examples of the contextual dependence of the application of the notion of literal meaning are easy to multiply. Consider the imperative sentence "Shut the door." As soon as we hear this sentence we are likely to picture a standard scene in which it would have a clear literal application. The speaker and hearer are in a room. The room has an open door that can be moved into its door frame and latches into the frame when closed. But as soon as we alter this domestic scene radically the sentence loses its application. Suppose the speaker and hearer are floating with a door in the middle of the ocean; or suppose they and the door are sitting alone in the Sahara. What are the obedience conditions of "Shut the door" in these situations? Still, one might say, though the literal meaning of the sentence loses its application in these mid-ocean and Sahara examples, such presuppositions as that there is a room and that the door is in the door frame do look like standard presuppositions for the obedience conditions of this sentence. They at least can be spelled out. But in answer to that: when we have spelled them out we are no better off. Suppose we are in our standard scene and the speaker utters the sentence "Shut the door", saying exactly and literally what he means. Suppose the hearer goes to the door and chops the entire complex – door, frame, hinges, latch and all – from the wall, sets the whole mess up in the middle of the room and then moves the door on its hinges so that it latches in the frame. Has he shut the door, that is, are the obedience conditions of the sentence satisfied? I am inclined to say that, as we look over our shoulder at the gaping hole he left in the wall, we would say no, the obedience conditions are not satisfied. But again, it would be very easy to vary the assumptions in such a way that we would say the obedience conditions of the sentence were satisfied. And there does not seem to be any upper limit on our ability to generate such deviant contexts. Suppose the hearer swallows the whole thing – wall, door, frame, and latch – and then moves the door into the door frame as part of the peristaltic contraction of his gut during digestion. Did he "shut the door"? Furthermore, the sentences that we used to state the presuppositions – that there is a room, that the room has walls, that at least one wall has a door opening with a door frame – will be just as subject to the sorts of contextual dependencies we designed them to eliminate as was our original sentence. Yet, for each of these examples, I want to say that the speaker says or can say exactly and literally what he means. There is no question of his being ambiguous, vague, or metaphorical when he says "Give me a hamburger ..." or "Shut the door"; but these literal utterances only determine a set of obedience conditions relative to a set of contextual assumptions. Different assumptions may determine different obedience conditions; and for some assumptions there may be no obedience conditions at all, even though, to repeat, the sentence and hence the utterance is perfectly unambiguous.

Indeed, the very terminology of "assumptions" and "contexts" might mislead if it suggests that for each sentence we could make all these assumptions explicit on the model of a set of axioms, as Peano and Frege tried to make explicit the assumptions of arithmetic, or as an economic theorist constructing a deductive economic model makes explicit his assumptions in the form of a set of axioms. But even assuming we could not do a sentence by sentence specification of the assumptions behind the understanding and application of each sentence, could we do a completely general specification of all the assumptions, all the things we take for granted, in our understanding of language? Could we make our whole mode of sensibility fully explicit? It seems to me that the arguments in this article don't determine the answer to that question one way or the other. The fact that for each of a large range of sentences the assumptions are variable and indefinite and that the specification of one will tend to bring in others does not by itself show that we could not specify an entire set which would be independent of the semantic analysis of individual sentences but which taken together would enable us to apply the literal meaning of sentences. The practical difficulties in any such specification would of course be prodigious, but is there any theoretical obstacle to the task? In order to show that there was we would have to show that the conditions under which sentences can represent were not themselves fully representable by sentences. Perhaps that claim is true but it has not been the aim of my discussion to show that it is true.

The claims that I have made about sentences lead naturally to our next conclusion: what I have said about literal meaning also applies to intentional states[3] in general. A man who believes that the cat is on the mat or who expects that they will bring him a medium rare hamburger has his belief and expectation only against a background of other inexplicit "assumptions". Just as the literal meaning of a sentence will determine different truth or obedience conditions relative to different sets of assumptions, so a belief or expectation will

---

[3] By "intentional states" here I mean those mental states such as belief and desire that are directed at or about objects and states of affairs in the world. They differ from such states as pains and tickles that are not in that way directed at or about anything.

have different conditions of satisfaction relative to different sets of assumptions. And it is really not surprising that there should be this parallelism between literal meaning and intentional states, since the notion of the literal meaning of a sentence is in a sense the notion of conventional and hence fungible intentionality: it is what enables the sentence to represent out there in public, so to speak; whereas my beliefs, desires, and expectations just represent their conditions of satisfaction *tout court*, regardless of whether they get any help from having public forms of expression. The general point is that representation, whether linguistic or otherwise, in general goes on against a background of assumptions which are not and in most cases could not also be completely represented as part of or as presuppositions of the representation, for the two reasons we have already stated: the assumptions are indefinite in number and any attempt to represent them will tend to bring in other assumptions. There is an obvious analogy with pictorial representation in this last consideration, because if one tries to depict the method of projection of one's picture in yet another picture, the second picture will also require an as yet undepicted method of projection.

III

It is important not to overstate the case that has been made so far. I have by no means demonstrated the contextual dependence of the applicability of the notion of the literal meaning of a sentence. Rather, I have offered a few examples together with some hints as to how we could generalize the phenomena discovered in those examples. Furthermore since the examples concern weird cases it is hard to be sure about our linguistic intuitions in describing them. But even assuming I am right about these examples perhaps we could find sentences for which there would be no such contextual dependency. Perhaps one might show, for example, that an arithmetical sentence such as "$3 + 4 = 7$" is not dependent on any contextual assumptions for the applicability of its literal meaning. Even here, however, it appears that certain assumptions about the nature of mathematical operations such as addition[4] must be made in order to apply the literal meaning of the sentence. But to this one might reply, in a logicist vein, that these assumptions are in a sense part of the meaning of the sentence. Such an argument would raise many of the traditional disputes in the philosophy of mathematics, and I shall not attempt to pursue them here. For the purposes of this discussion, it is sufficient to argue that the notion of absolutely context free literal meaning does not have general application to sentences; and indeed there does seem to be a very large class of sentences to which we could extend the sorts of arguments for the contextual dependence of the applicability of literal meaning that we discussed earlier.

There are two skeptical conclusions that these reflections might seem to imply that I want to renounce explicitly. First, I am not saying that sentences do not have literal meanings. To show that a phenomenon X can only be identified relative to another phenomenon Y does not show that X does not exist. To take an obvious analogy, when one says that the notion of the movement of a body only has application relative to some coordinate system, one is not denying the existence of motion. Motion, though relative, is still motion. Similarly, when I say that the literal meaning of a sentence only has application relative to the coordinate system of our background assumptions, I am not denying that sentences have literal meanings. Literal meaning, though relative, is still literal meaning.

Well then, what is meant by "application" when I say that the literal meaning of a sentence only has "application" relative to a set of background assumptions? Simply this. There are certain jobs that we want the notion of meaning to do for us; it connects in all sorts of systematic ways with our theory of language and with our pretheoretical beliefs about language. Meaning is tied to our notions of truth conditions, entailment, inconsistency, understanding, and a host of other semantic and mental notions. Now the thesis of the relativity of meaning is the thesis that one can only make these

---

[4] Thus in Wittgenstein's example $A = 3$, $B = 4$, but $A + B = 5$

connections relative to some coordinate system of background assumptions. In the case, for example, of truth conditions (or obedience conditions for imperative sentences) the thesis of the relativity of meaning has the consequence that the sentence may determine one set of truth conditions relative to one set of assumptions and another set relative to another set of assumptions even though the sentence is not ambiguous and the variation is not a matter of indexical dependence (analogously, the thesis of the relativity of motion has the consequence that the same object at the same time may be moving one way relative to one coordinate system and the other way relative to another coordinate system even though it is not moving in two different ways), and without some set of background assumptions the sentence does not determine a definite set of truth conditions at all. For most sentences of the "Cat is on the mat", "Bill is in the kitchen", "My car has a flat tire" variety, the background assumptions are so fundamental and so pervasive that we don't see them at all. It takes a conscious effort to prise them off and examine them, and, incidentally, when one does prise them off it tends to produce an enormous sense of annoyance and insecurity in philosophers, linguists, and psychologists – or at any rate such has been my experience.

A second skeptical conclusion that I explicitly renounce is that the thesis of the relativity of literal meaning destroys or is in some way inconsistent with the system of distinctions presented in my brief summary of the standard account of meaning at the beginning of this chapter, namely that system of distinctions that centers around the distinction between the literal sentence meaning and the speaker's utterance meaning, where the utterance meaning may depart in various ways from literal sentence meaning. The distinction, for example, between literal sentence meaning and metaphorical or ironical utterance meaning remains intact. Similarly, the distinction between direct and indirect speech acts remains intact. The modification that the thesis of the relativity of meaning forces on that system of distinctions is that in the account of how context plays a role in the production and comprehension of metaphorical utterances, indirect speech acts, ironical utterances, and conversational implications, we will need to distinguish the special role of the context of utterance in these cases from the role that background assumptions play in the interpretation of literal meaning. Furthermore there is nothing in the thesis of the relativity of literal meaning which is inconsistent with the Principle of Expressibility, the principle that whatever can be meant can be said. It is not part of, nor a consequence of, my argument for the relativity of literal meaning that there are meanings that are inherently inexpressible.

In the face of these examples to support the thesis of the relativity of literal meaning, defenders of the traditional theory of absolute literal meaning are likely to resort to certain standard moves and it is perhaps well to obviate these before they can even get started. Neither the sentence–utterance distinction (much less the type–token distinction) nor the performance–competence distinction will rescue the thesis of absolutely context free literal meaning as far as our counterexamples are concerned. The discussion throughout has been about sentences, and I have discussed the meaning of utterances only in cases where utterance meaning coincides with sentence meaning, that is, only in cases where the speaker means literally what he says. Furthermore I have been discussing the understanding of the literal meaning of a sentence by a speaker as part of the speaker's semantic competence. The thesis I have been advancing is that for a large class of sentences the speaker, as part of his linguistic competence, knows how to apply the literal meaning of a sentence only against a background of other assumptions. If I am right, this argument has the consequence that there is no sharp distinction between a speaker's linguistic competence and his knowledge of the world, but there are numerous other arguments to support that position anyway. I have frequently made use of arguments of the form "What would we say if . . . ?" but that does not mean that we are not discussing sentence meanings or that we are not discussing linguistic competence.

Why should things be the way I have described them,

assuming for the sake of argument that my description is correct? That is, for example, why couldn't we just lay it down that the meaning of the sentence "The cat is on the mat" or "That door is shut" was going to be absolutely context free? Meanings are, after all, a matter of convention, and if heretofore such conventions have rested on background assumptions why not put an end to this dependence by a new convention that there shall henceforth be no such dependence? I don't know how to answer these questions except by saying that literal meaning is dependent on context in the same way that other non-conventional forms of intentionality are dependent on context, and there is no way to eliminate the dependence in the case of literal meaning which would not break the connections with other forms of intentionality and hence would eliminate the intentionality of literal meaning altogether.

Since perception is in all likelihood the primary form of intentionality, the one on which all others depend, we can best begin by showing the contextual dependency of the applicability of the contents of our perceptions. Consider the characteristic visual experiences that would be present when we are in a position to say "I see that the cat is on the mat." As far as the purely qualitative visual aspects of these experiences are concerned (and I don't know a better vocabulary than "qualitative visual aspects" to get at what I am talking about) many of these aspects could have been produced by any number of causes and in any number of situations. They might have been produced by stimulating the optical centers of my brain in such a way as to give me experiences with visual aspects just like the aspects I have in my present visual experiences. Yet I want to say that my present visual experiences, the ones that enable me to say that I see that the cat is on the mat, have a form of intentionality that these other experiences would not have, assuming that is that I knew what was going on in the two cases. In my present experience I assume that I am perceiving the cat and the mat from a certain point of view where my body is located; I assume that these visual experiences are causally dependent on the state of affairs that I perceive; I assume that I am not standing on my head and seeing cat and mat upside down, etc.; and all these assumptions are in addition to such general assumptions as that I am in a gravitational field, there are no wires attaching to cat and mat, etc. Now, the intentionality of the visual experience will determine a set of conditions of satisfaction. But the purely visual aspects of the experience will produce a set of conditions of satisfaction only against a set of background assumptions which are not themselves part of the visual experience. I don't for example see the point of view from which I see that the cat is on the mat and I don't see the gravitational field within which they are both located. Yet the conditions of satisfaction which are determined by the content of my perception are in part dependent on such assumptions. Indeed in this case as in the literal meaning case, the intentionality of the visual perception only has an application, only determines a set of conditions of satisfaction, against some system of background assumptions. Thus there seems no way to eliminate the contextual dependence of literal meaning since it is built into other forms of intentionality on which literal meaning depends. To borrow an expression from Wittgenstein, it is part of the grammar of "The cat is on the mat" that this is what we call "seeing that the cat is on the mat", "believing that the cat is on the mat", etc. There is no way to eliminate the contextual dependence of the sentence "The cat is on the mat" without breaking the connections between that sentence and the *perception* that the cat is on the mat, or the belief that the cat is on the mat, and it is on such connections that the meaning of the sentence depends.

Chapter 6

REFERENTIAL AND ATTRIBUTIVE

Is there a distinction between referential and attributive uses of definite descriptions? I think most philosophers who approach Donnellan's distinction (Donnellan, 1966 and 1968) from the point of view of the theory of speech acts, those who see reference as a type of speech act, would say that there is no such distinction and that the cases he presents can be accounted for as instances of the general distinction between speaker meaning and sentence meaning: both alleged uses are referential in the sense that they are cases of referring to objects, the only difference is in the degree to which the speaker makes his intentions fully explicit in his utterance. Such objections are in fact quite commonly made, both in the literature and in the oral tradition, but I have never seen a version of the objection I was fully satisfied with and the main aim of this chapter is to attempt to provide one.

I. DONNELLAN'S ACCOUNT OF THE DISTINCTION

Donnellan presents the distinction by means of certain examples, which we are supposed to be able to generalize. Suppose we come across the battered body of Smith, murdered by someone unknown to us. We might say, "Smith's murderer is insane", meaning by "Smith's murderer" not any particular person but, rather, *whoever it was* that murdered Smith. This is the attributive use. But now suppose in the courtroom scene where Jones is on trial for the murder of Smith, observing his strange behavior we might say, "Smith's murderer is insane", meaning by "Smith's murderer", that man over there in the dock, Jones, who is behaving so strangely. In this case we don't mean *whoever* murdered Smith, we mean a *particular* man, the one we see in front of us. This is the referential use. A crucial feature of the distinction is that in the referential uses it doesn't matter if the definite description we use is actually true of the object we are referring to. Suppose that the man in front of us did not actually murder Smith, suppose no one murdered Smith but that he committed suicide, still in some sense at least, according to Donnellan, our statement would be true if the man we are referring to is insane. In the referential use, since we are just using the expression to pick out some object about which we then go on to say something truly or falsely it doesn't matter if the expression is true of the object. But in the attributive use, if our definite description is true of nothing, our statement cannot be true. If no one murdered Smith our statement cannot be true. Donnellan then objects to both Russell's and Strawson's theories of definite descriptions on the grounds that they both fail to account for the referential use.

Intuitively there does seem to be a distinction between these cases. What exactly is it? Donnellan nowhere gives us a set of necessary and sufficient conditions for identifying each use but he does offer the following as a summary of the distinction as it applies to assertions:[1]

> If a speaker S uses a definite description, "the ϕ", referentially there will be some entity e (or, at least, the speaker will intend that there should be) about which the following will be true . . .
>
> (1) S will have referred to e whether or not e is in fact ϕ.
>
> (2) S will have said something true or false about e whether or not e is in fact ϕ (provided that everything is in order concerning the remainder of the speech act).
>
> (3) S, in using "the ϕ" to refer to e, will have presupposed or implied that e is ϕ.
>
> (4) In reporting S's speech act, it will be correct to say that he stated something about e and in reporting this to

---

[1] (Donnellan, 1968, p. 206) Donnellan confines his discussion mostly to statements (as I will in this chapter) but the theory is intended to apply *mutatis mutandis* to other sorts of speech acts as well.

use expressions to refer to *e* other than the "the ϕ" or synonyms of it.

Had the definite description been used attributively there would be no such entity *e* (nor would the speaker have intended that there should be).

Now it turns out that this characterization isn't quite right even on Donnellan's own terms because it is immediately subject to certain sorts of counterexamples, which Donnellan recognizes but does not regard as a serious challenge to his theory. Suppose that Smith died of natural causes but just before his death he was assaulted and it was the evidence of this assault that led us to attribute insanity to "Smith's murderer." Here we might say that our statement was true even though nothing satisfies the definite description "Smith's murderer." That is, in this attributive use we have a case which satisfies our conditions (1)–(4) above for the referential use, and so the distinction seems to be threatened. If we plug in "the murderer" for "the ϕ" and "the assailant" for "*e*" in the above formulae (1)–(4) this case satisfies all the conditions for being referential yet it is supposed to be attributive. How can we account for these sorts of examples and still keep the distinction intact? Donnellan's answer is that this sort of a case is a "near miss" and that such cases are still quite different from genuine referential uses: "A near miss occurs with an attributive use when nothing exactly fits the description used, but some individual or other does fit a description in some sense close in meaning to the one used. It is a quite different sort of 'near miss', however, that is recognized by seeing that the particular individual the speaker wanted to refer to has been described in a slightly inaccurate way" (1968, p. 209). Only in the referential cases can we "miss by a mile".

Still, the counterexamples remain a bit worrisome because at the very least we should be able to go back and rewrite conditions (1)–(4) so as to exclude these near miss attributive cases from qualifying as referential and it is not at all easy to see how to do that without using question begging formulations such as "close in meaning" or "near miss".

However, at this point I am trying to present Donnellan's case in the strongest possible light and not to make objections to it. In discussing the counterexamples he introduces the following metaphor. In the referential use the speaker is aiming at a particular target, and he can be aiming at that target even if he misses it narrowly or misses it by a mile (his statement can be true of the object he is referring to even if the definite description is a near miss or is wildly inaccurate). But in the attributive case he is not aiming at a particular target; he is aiming at "some target or other" (his statement can be true only if he hits the target or scores a near miss). "Once this is seen, taking near misses into account does not blur the distinction. If anything it helps one to see what the distinction is" (1968, p. 210).

Furthermore, Donnellan is anxious to insist that the distinction is not simply a distinction between the number of beliefs that the speaker and hearer have about the object, if any, which satisfies the definite description. It is not merely a distinction between having a lot of beliefs about Smith's murderer in the referential case and having few in the attributive case, because even in the case where I have a lot of beliefs I can use the definite description attributively. Thus suppose I have a whole lot of beliefs about the man who I suppose won the Indianapolis 500: I believe that his name is Brown, that he is my brother-in-law, etc. Still I might make a bet expressed by the sentence "The man who won the Indianapolis 500 drove a turbine-powered car." And here I am not using the expression referentially even though I have a whole lot of beliefs about the man who I suppose satisfies it. This is proven by the fact that I might win the bet even if my brother-in-law is not the winner of the race and I might lose the bet even if he was driving a turbine-powered car, for I will win the bet if and only if the winner, whoever he is, was driving a turbine-powered car.

These last sorts of examples lead Donnellan to make what I believe is his most ambitious claim, relating to condition 4 above: In the attributive use the speaker is not really *referring* at all. Or to put it in the formal mode, in the attributive use, we in reporting his attributive use of "the ϕ" where e satisfies "the φ" cannot say that he referred to *e* or even that he *referred* to anything at all. To substantiate this claim, consider the following sort of example. Suppose that in 1960 someone had predicted on the basis of a knowledge of Republican politics, "The Republican presidential candidate in 1964 will be a conservative." Now since Goldwater, a conservative, eventually got the 1964 nomination the statement was true and the definite description used attributively was true of Goldwater. In Russell's terms it would be correct to say that the definite description *denotes* Goldwater, nonetheless according to Donnellan the speaker did not *refer to* Goldwater, nor indeed did he refer (in the sense of picking out or identifying some object) to anyone, because he didn't know who was going to be the presidential candidate, and what he meant was *whoever* is the presidential candidate will be a conservative. In the referential use, on the other hand, the speaker *has in mind* some specific object or person, and it is for this reason that we can say in reporting his speech act that he *referred* to that object or person.

There are three features of Donnellan's account that it seems to me any rival account must deal with:

1. There just seems to be an intuitively obvious difference between the referential and the attributive cases. This intuition must be accounted for.

2. Our intuitions are supported by the fact that utterances of sentences containing referential uses apparently have different truth conditions from utterances containing attributive uses. What more proof of ambiguity could one ask for?

3. There is further syntactical support for making the distinction in that the attributive uses seem to admit the insertion of "whoever" or "whatever" clauses, e.g. "Smith's murderer, whoever he is, is insane."

II. AN ALTERNATIVE ACCOUNT

The simplest way for me to discuss the foregoing account is to present an alternative explanation and show why I believe it is superior to Donnellan's account.

How is it possible for speakers to refer to objects at all? Reference is achieved with a variety of syntactical devices, among them proper names, definite descriptions and pronouns, including demonstrative pronouns. And speakers will be able to use these devices to refer to objects in virtue of standing in certain relations to the objects. For example, a speaker might know the proper name of the object, or he might know some facts about the object, or he might be able to see it in his field of vision, or he might be sitting on top of it, etc. Now there are a number of different theories in philosophy about how these various relations in which speakers stand to objects enable them to refer to objects using these various syntactical devices. It is not my aim in this article to continue the arguments between these various theories, so I will try to adopt a terminology which is neutral between them.[2] Since all these theories agree that there must be some linguistic device that the speaker uses to refer to the object, we can say that whenever a speaker refers he must have some linguistic representation of the object – a proper name, a definite description, etc. – and this representation will represent the object referred to under some *aspect* or other. An utterance of "Smith's murderer" represents an object under the aspect of being Smith's murderer, "Jones" represents an object under the aspect of being Jones, "that man over there" represents an object under the aspect of being that man over there, etc. I think some of these "aspects", such as those whose expression involves proper names, are subject to further analysis; but since I am seeking a neutral terminology here and not attempting to defend any specific theory of reference or of proper names, we can ignore this problem for present purposes. We can simply say that all reference is under an aspect, that this is a consequence of the

[2] Perhaps in the end it will prove impossible to get a completely neutral terminology, one that is neutral between the various theories of reference. But as Donnellan does not present the referential–attributive distinction as dependent on the rest of his theory of reference, the fact that the terminology I shall employ in discussing his distinction may not sit comfortably with the rest of his theory of reference should not prevent us from making a fair examination of the distinction as he presents it. My aim in this chapter is to examine the referential–attributive distinction and not his whole theory of reference.

point on which all theories agree, namely that reference always involves a linguistic representation of the object referred to, and for present purposes this will enable us to admit not only such aspects as being Smith's murderer or being that man over there, but even being Jones or being called "Jones". We can also allow that in cases of linguistic ignorance the aspect the speaker intends might not be accurately expressed by the expression he utters; for example he might erroneously suppose that Smith's name was pronounced "Schmidt" and thus when he uttered the expression "Schmidt's murderer" he was actually referring under the aspect "Smith's murderer", since that is the aspect he intended by his linguistic representation even though he did not know the correct way to express that aspect. Such cases have to be distinguished from genuine cases of mistaken identity where there really is a confusion of aspects.

There is a familiar distinction in the philosophy of language between what a sentence or an expression means and what a speaker means when he utters that sentence or expression. The interest of the distinction derives not from the relatively trivial fact that the speaker may be ignorant of the meaning of the sentence or expression, but from the fact that even where the speaker has perfect linguistic competence the literal sentence or expression meaning may not coincide with the speaker's utterance meaning. Some of the standard examples of this divergence are metaphor, where the speaker says one thing but means something else, irony where the speaker says one thing but means the opposite of what he says, and indirect speech acts where the speaker says one thing, means what he says, but also means something more. In my account of indirect speech acts (Searle, 1975b, chapter 2 of this volume), I distinguish between the speaker's primary illocutionary act which is not literally expressed in his utterance and his secondary illocutionary act, which is literally expressed. The primary illocutionary act is performed indirectly by way of performing the secondary illocutionary act. Thus for example I might request a man to get off my foot by saying, "You are standing on my foot." In such cases I literally make a statement to the effect that the man is standing on my foot, but I don't just do that. My illocutionary intentions include the meaning of the sentence I utter but they go beyond it, because I mean not only: you are standing on my foot, but also: please get off my foot. In such cases one performs two speech acts in one utterance, because the primary illocutionary act of requesting the man to get off my foot is performed indirectly by way of performing the secondary illocutionary act of stating that he is on my foot. Now exactly how one performs the primary by way of performing the secondary is fairly complicated, but that such things commonly occur should be obvious even from this one example.

What is going on in Donnellan's so-called referential cases is simply this. Sometimes when one refers to an object one is in possession of a whole lot of aspects under which or in virtue of which one could have referred to that object, but one picks out one aspect under which one refers to the object. Usually the aspect one picks out will be one that the speaker supposes will enable the hearer to pick out the same object. In such cases, as in the indirect speech act cases, one means what one says but one means something more as well. In these cases any aspect will do, provided it enables the hearer to pick out the object. (It may even be something which both the hearer and speaker believe to be false of the object, as in the case presented by Donnellan where speaker and hearer refer to a man as "the King" even though they believe he is a usurper.) Thus, one says "Smith's murderer" but means also: that man over there, Jones, the one accused of the crime, the person now being cross-examined by the district attorney, the one who is behaving so strangely, and so on. In such cases if the aspect one picked out to refer to the object doesn't work one can fall back on some other aspect. *But notice that in every "referential" use, though the expression actually used may be false of the object referred to and thus the object does not satisfy the aspect under which it is referred to, there must always be some other aspect under which the speaker could have referred to the object and which is satisfied by the object. Furthermore, this aspect is such that if nothing satisfies it the statement cannot be true.* For example, consider the referential use of the definite description in

"Smith's murderer is insane", said of a man both speaker and hearer are looking at. Now they might agree that the speaker had made a true statement about *that man*, the one they are looking at even though neither he nor anyone else satisfies the definite description "Smith's murderer". So let us suppose that the speaker falls back on the aspect expressed by "the man we are both looking at". "Yes," he says, "when I said 'Smith's murderer' I was referring to the man we were both looking at. That's the man I meant, whether or not he murdered Smith." But now suppose they are not looking at anybody, that the whole experience was a hallucination. Can we still claim that what the speaker said was true? Well, we might, provided that the speaker can fall back on yet another aspect. He might say, "Even though nobody murdered Smith and we weren't looking at anybody, the man I really had in mind is the one accused by the District Attorney of murdering Smith. I was saying of that man that he was insane." But now suppose nobody satisfies the aspect expressed by "being the one accused by the District Attorney of murdering Smith". We might repeat the same procedure and get yet another aspect, but eventually we will reach bedrock. That is, eventually we will reach an aspect such that if no one satisfies it the statement cannot be true and if one person satisfies it the statement will be true or false depending on whether that person is insane. And indeed it seems to me that this point can be generalized to all of Donnellan's examples of "referential" uses of definite descriptions: provided that the speaker's intentions are clear enough so that we can say that he really knew what he meant, then even though the aspect expressed by the expression he utters may not be satisfied by the object he "had in mind" or may not be satisfied by anything, still there must be some aspect (or collection of aspects) such that if nothing satisfies it (or them) the statement cannot be true and if some one thing satisfies it the statement will be true or false depending on whether or not the thing that satisfies it has the property ascribed to it. Pursuing the analogy with my account of indirect speech acts, I propose to call this the *primary* aspect under which reference is made and contrast it with the *secondary* aspect. If nothing satisfies the primary aspect the speaker didn't have anything in mind, he only thought he did, and consequently his statement cannot be true. The secondary aspect is any aspect which the speaker expresses in a definite description (or other expression) and which is such that the speaker utters it in an attempt to secure reference to the object which satisfies his primary aspect, but which is not itself intended as part of the truth conditions of the statement he is attempting to make. It follows from these accounts that for every secondary aspect there must be a primary aspect, and this is true of all of Donnellan's examples: every "referential" use is an utterance of a definite description which expresses a secondary aspect and every "referential" use has an underlying primary aspect. Thus consider the following example from Donnellan. I might say "That man over there with champagne in his glass is happy." But suppose the man over there only had water in his glass; still what I said might be true of *that man over there* even though the definite description I used to identify him is not true of him. The primary aspect is expressed by "that man over there", the secondary aspect is expressed by "that man over there with champagne in his glass". The secondary aspect does not figure in the truth conditions (except insofar as it includes the primary aspect), the primary aspect does figure in the truth conditions: if nothing satisfies the aspect of being that man over there the statement cannot be true. All of Donnellan's referential cases are simply cases where the speaker uses a definite description that expresses a secondary aspect under which reference is made. But the fact that a definite description can be uttered to express either a secondary or a primary aspect no more shows that there is an ambiguity in definite descriptions, or that there are two different uses of definite descriptions, than the fact that one can utter the sentence "You are standing on my foot" either in a secondary illocutionary act, to request someone to get off my foot, or in a primary act, just to state that he is standing on my foot, shows that the sentence is ambiguous or that it has two distinct uses.

Just as in the indirect speech act cases one performs the

primary illocutionary act by way of performing the literal secondary illocutionary act, so in the referential use of definite descriptions one performs the act of referring to an object as satisfying the primary aspect by way of performing an act of reference expressing a secondary aspect. In both cases one's communication intentions will succeed if one's hearer grasps the primary intention on the basis of hearing the expression which expresses the secondary intention. And in both cases one can succeed in one's primary intent even in certain cases where one's secondary speech act is defective in various ways. I can succeed in requesting you to get off my foot by saying "You're standing on my foot" even though you are not standing on my foot but sitting on it, and I can succeed in referring to the man we are both looking at by saying "Smith's murderer" even though neither he nor anyone else murdered Smith.

The requirement that every referential statement must have a primary aspect is simply the requirement that every such statement must have a specifiable content. If the utterance of "Smith's murderer is insane" is supposed to constitute the making of a true statement even though the person referred to is not Smith's murderer then the content of the statement must be different from the meaning of the sentence. The content of the statement cannot be expressed by "Smith's murderer is insane" for the statement can be true even though there is no "Smith's murderer". What then is the content of the statement? The answer to that question will specify the primary aspect. The specification of the statement being made – as opposed to the specification of the sentence uttered – will have to specify that aspect under which reference is made that actually counts in the truth conditions of the statement. This is an immediate consequence of the requirement that if the statement is true there must be some possible specification of exactly what statement it is that is true. And that there are two distinct reference acts being performed in these cases, a primary and a secondary, is shown by the fact that my hearer upon hearing me say in the so-called referential case "Smith's murderer is insane" can respond to my utterance by saying, "You are right in saying that the man we are both looking at is insane, but you are wrong in thinking he is Smith's murderer." In such a response the hearer accepts the statement I am making under the primary aspect, but rejects the attribution of the secondary aspect (expressed by "Smith's murderer") to the object referred to under the primary aspect (expressed by "the man we are both looking at").

This distinction between primary and secondary aspects also applies to proper names. Suppose I say, "In *Hamlet*, Shakespeare develops the character of Hamlet much more convincingly than he develops the character of Ophelia." Now suppose that Shakespeare didn't write *Hamlet*, suppose that of all the plays attributed to him, it alone was in fact written by someone else. Is my statement false? Not necessarily, for by "Shakespeare" I may simply have meant the author of *Hamlet*. "Shakespeare" may have expressed a secondary aspect, and the primary aspect may have been "author of *Hamlet*" and what I meant was, and hence the statement I made was, "the author of *Hamlet* develops the character of Hamlet more convincingly than he develops the character of Ophelia" and that statement, like Donnellan's examples of referential uses of definite descriptions, can be true even though it was not expressed exactly by the sentence I uttered, and the statement made using only the aspect expressed by the sentence I uttered would be false.

What is going on in the so-called attributive uses of definite descriptions is simply this: the expression uttered expresses the primary aspect under which reference is made. Thus the statement made cannot be true if nothing satisfies that aspect, and if one object satisfies that aspect the statement will be true or false depending on whether or not the object that satisfies that aspect has the property ascribed to it. In the attributive cases in short, speaker meaning and sentence meaning are the same. And in Donnellan's examples the expression uttered must express a primary aspect for one of two reasons. Either it is the only aspect in possession of the speaker (the "attributive" example of the Smith's murder case) and consequently it is the only aspect under which the speaker can secure reference, or in those cases where the speaker is in possession of several aspects under which he could secure reference (e.g. the winner of the race case) only one of them figures crucially in the satisfaction conditions of the speech act he is performing, and that is the one he utters. Let us consider each of these cases in turn.

When we find Smith's mutilated body but have no knowledge of the identity of the murderer we have no (or very few) aspects to refer to the person about whom we wish to predicate insanity except "the murderer". Leaving aside the "near miss" cases, there is no plausible way for our utterance meaning to differ from sentence meaning because no other aspect could function as primary aspect. To see this consider a variation on Donnellan's example. Suppose that just prior to stumbling on Smith's body I, but not you, see a man running from the scene. You say, on seeing the body, "Smith's murderer is insane." I say "Yes, he certainly is insane" or even "Yes, Smith's murderer certainly is insane." Now, contrary to Donnellan, I want to argue that both your "Smith's murderer" and my "he" and my "Smith's murderer" are used to refer. Furthermore, they are used to refer under the same aspect. But your expression expresses a primary aspect, and mine may or may not express a primary aspect; I may also have meant "the man I just saw running away" and I may have meant to attribute insanity to him even if it turns out that he is not responsible for the death of Smith. I have two aspects either of which could be primary. You have only one aspect and since all referential statements have a primary aspect it must be the primary aspect of your statement.

In the bet on the outcome of the car race the speaker has a whole series of aspects but only one can be primary because only one is relevant to the satisfaction conditions of the bet. It would be possible to make the same bet using a secondary aspect to refer to the winner, provided that the speaker and hearer knew that the interest in referring to him was only that he was the winner and that the bet was being made under that aspect. Thus if you and I are both looking at the man we suppose won the race I might make the same bet by saying "I bet that guy was driving a turbine-powered car." Here "that guy" expresses a secondary aspect and "the winner of the Indianapolis 500" expresses the primary aspect. The case satisfies Donnellan's tests for being referential since the person I really "had in mind" was the winner of the race, regardless of whether or not he is "that guy".

We can now summarize the differences between my account and Donnellan's. On his account there are two distinct uses of definite descriptions only one of which is a use to refer. Definite descriptions thus have an ambiguity, though he allows that it may be a "pragmatic" and not a "semantic" ambiguity.[3] On my account there is no such ambiguity. According to me all of his cases are cases where the definite description is used to refer. The only difference is that in the so-called referential cases the reference is made under a secondary aspect, and in the so-called attributive cases it is made under a primary aspect. Since every statement containing a reference must have a primary aspect, in the "referential" use the speaker may still have referred to something that satisfies the primary aspect even though the expression uttered, which expresses a secondary aspect, is not true of that object and may not be true of anything. Whether or not the utterance of a sentence to make a statement contains a definite description used as a primary aspect or a secondary aspect depends on the intentions of the speaker; that is, it is a matter of the statement he is making and not just of the sentence he utters.

Well, what about Donnellan's stronger claim that the attributive use does not refer at all? The intuitive basis for this claim is that in such cases as my saying in 1960 "The Republican candidate in 1964 will be a conservative", I cannot have been referring to Goldwater because I had no idea who the Republican candidate would be. There was, to

---

[3] It is not at all clear, by the way, what a "pragmatic ambiguity" is supposed to be. "I went to the bank" is semantically ambiguous. "Flying planes can be dangerous" is syntactically ambiguous. But what is a pragmatic ambiguity? Is "You are standing on my foot" supposed to be pragmatically ambiguous because in some contexts its utterance can be more than just a statement of fact? If so, then every sentence is indefinitely "pragmatically ambiguous". If we had a notion of "pragmatic ambiguity" we would also have to have a notion of "pragmatic univocality" but in fact neither notion has any clear sense at all.

use Donnellan's metaphor, no particular target I was aiming at, hence I was not referring to anybody. I on the other hand want to maintain that I was indeed referring, I was referring to the Republican candidate in 1964. Now since I did not know which of the various possible people was going to be the Republican candidate, I did not know which of them I was referring to. The primary aspect of my reference was expressed by "Republican candidate in 1964" and I had no other aspects under which I could refer. But these facts do not show that my utterance was not referential. To see this, imagine that I now say, "Yes, I was right way back there in 1960 when I predicted that the Republican candidate in 1964 would be a conservative, for the Republican candidate in 1964 was indeed a conservative." It seems to me that my earlier utterances of "the Republican candidate in 1964" are no more and no less referential than my later utterances. In both cases I was referring to the person who is in fact Goldwater, though in 1960 I had no way of knowing that. The main obstacle to seeing this point is the fact that, as Donnellan points out, when a person uses an expression of the form "the ϕ" to refer, even assuming that the ϕ is identical with e, we cannot always plausibly report his speech act by saying that he referred to e. Even where we know that Goldwater was the Republican presidential candidate in 1964, we can't always report his utterance of a sentence containing "the Republican presidential candidate of 1964" by saying "he referred to Goldwater". Whereas it seems in the so-called referential cases such reports are often justified. If he uttered a sentence containing "Smith's murderer" and we know that the man he had in mind was Jones we can report his speech act in the form, "He referred to Jones" and we can do this not only in cases where Smith's murderer is identical to Jones but even in cases where Jones is not Smith's murderer.

I believe that these facts have a fairly simple explanation in terms of the analysis offered earlier together with the fact that sentences of the form "S referred to x" and those of the form "S said that x is P" are intensional contexts. Substitution of expressions normally used to refer to the same object is not in general a valid form of inference for intensional contexts. The reason we are inclined to think there is a difference between the so-called attributive and referential cases is that in the referential cases we know that the speaker has several aspects in hand under which he could have referred to the referent and we are more willing to report his speech act under one of the other aspects than we are in the "attributive" cases. If he says "Smith's murderer is insane" and we know that he knows or believes that Smith's murderer is Jones then we are more willing to report his speech act in the form, "He said that Jones was insane", than if he didn't know who Smith's murderer was when he made his statement. Indeed if we know the primary aspect under which the reference was made it will in general be correct to report his statement under that aspect (regardless of the expression he actually used and regardless of whether the expression he actually used is true of the object that satisfies his primary aspect) since that reports the referential content of the statement he was making. In fact reports of both of the so-called referential and attributive occurrences have both intensional and extensional readings. Thus if Jones is the murderer and his friends hear that the Sheriff has said "attributively" "Smith's murderer is insane" they might well report this to Jones as "The Sheriff says that you are insane." Similarly there are substitutions of aspects in the so-called referential cases which would be unwarranted. Thus suppose someone in 1910 says to Goldwater's mother about the then infant Goldwater, "Mrs. Goldwater, your youngest son wants more milk." Now it is easy to imagine that this could be a "referential" use. It might turn out that baby Goldwater was not the youngest son and still the speaker knew who he was talking about. All the same it would sound distinctly odd to say that the speaker was referring to the Republican presidential candidate of 1964 or to report his speech act by saying that he said the Republican presidential candidate of 1964 wanted more milk. But all of these facts have to do with quite familiar features of intensional contexts, deriving from the fact that when we report someone's reference we are often in varying degrees committed to reporting the aspects under which the reference was made. They do not show that in the so-called attributive cases the speaker is not referring. What they do show is that since all reference is under some aspect or other it may be misleading or even downright false to report a reference to an object under an aspect that the speaker did not in fact use and could not have used because he had no way of knowing that the object satisfying the aspects under which he did refer also satisfied the other aspect.

III. SOME RESIDUAL PROBLEMS

1. Whoever *and* whatever

What about the "whoever" test? Doesn't the fact that the attributive uses naturally take "whoever", "whichever" and "whatever" clauses show that there is something to the distinction beyond the distinction between primary and secondary aspects? I think not. To begin with, cases that are clearly "referential" (i.e. made under secondary aspects) can also take these clauses as in, e.g., "That man over there in the funny hat, whoever he is, is trying to break into our car!" Now the case is clearly "referential" for it might not be a man in a funny hat but for example a woman with a strange hairdo. The applicability of these interrogative pronouns, like the notion of knowing who (or what) someone (or something) is, will always be relative to some set of interests in the context of the utterance. For example, relative to one set of interests I know who Heidegger is, relative to another set I do not. If you ask me, "Who is Klaus Heidegger?", I can say for example, "He is the Austrian slalom specialist who finished second to Stenmark in the 1977 World Cup competition"; but relative to some other sets of interests I haven't the faintest idea who he is. I couldn't pick him out of a police lineup or tell you any of the salient facts of his life, for example. And indeed when Heidegger suddenly burst on the scene in 1977 it would have been quite appropriate to say, e.g., "This guy Heidegger, whoever he is, has won yet another race." In this case as in the earlier cases, the use of "whoever" ("whatever", "whichever") indicates ignorance of, doubts about, or suspension of other aspects than the one which is expressed in the sentence. Such uses can occur more commonly with primary aspects, both because we often don't know any other aspects (as in, e.g., the "attributive", i.e. primary, use of "Smith's murderer") or when we do know of other aspects we can make it clear that they are suspended for the purpose of the utterance, they are not part of its content (as in, e.g., "I bet the winner of the race, whoever he was, used a turbine-powered car").

2. *The attributive near misses*

We are now in a position to see what is going on in the near miss cases discussed by Donnellan. It is very unrealistic to talk, as I have been talking, as if our beliefs about the world and the aspects under which we refer to objects came in neat little packages which we could label primary or secondary aspect. In fact our beliefs come in whole messy networks, and in any situation in which we are likely to be able on the basis of observation to use an expression such as "Smith's murderer" to refer, we are also likely to have a whole lot of other aspects. Thus "Smith's assailant", "the person who left this weapon at the scene of the crime", "the person responsible for these footprints at the scene of the crime" – and so on – would be possible candidates for expressing other aspects under which reference could have been made, since it is unlikely that we could have any observational evidence that there was anyone to be referred to as "Smith's murderer" unless we had the sort of evidence that would enable us to refer under some of these other aspects. Even in the "attributive" cases, we are likely to have a collection of aspects under which reference could be made, and should any one of them fail us we can fall back on the others, just as we do in the "referential" cases; for what we really had in mind was, e.g., "the person responsible for what we observed". There is therefore no sharp dividing line between referring under a primary or a secondary aspect. As long as all goes well the question would not normally arise. Only if there is some breakdown, if for example it turns out that Smith wasn't really murdered but only assaulted, would we be forced to specify exactly what we meant, what our primary aspect was.

3. Speaker reference and semantic reference

Kripke (1977) approaches Donnellan's distinction with an apparatus somewhat like mine, but it seems to me his account gets bogged down, and it may be instructive to say exactly how. He says that the distinction is between *speaker reference* and *semantic reference*. In the attributive case speaker reference and semantic reference coincide because the speaker's intention is just to refer to the semantic reference and in the referential case the speaker's reference and the semantic reference may coincide if, as the speaker believes, they both determine the same object, but they need not; if the speaker is mistaken, the semantic reference may be different from the speaker's reference (p. 264). Kripke's account couldn't be quite right as it stands, because in the "referential" use the speaker need not even believe that the object referred to satisfies the description he uses, as Donnellan's example of referring to a usurper as "The King" illustrates. However, the distinction between speaker reference and semantic reference looks like the familiar distinction I use between speaker meaning and sentence meaning, though Kripke adopts an odd way of putting it, since reference, unlike meaning, is a speech act. In the sense in which speakers refer, expressions do not refer any more than they make promises or give orders. Still, one could explain away this difficulty very easily if one analyzed "semantic reference" in terms of aspects determined by literal meaning. Kripke starts off as if he is going to do that (p. 263) but he then goes on to try to analyze both speaker's reference and semantic reference in terms of different kinds of intentions: "In a given idiolect the semantic reference of a designator (without indexicals) is given by a *general* intention of the speaker to refer to a certain object whenever the designator is used. The speaker's referent is given by a *specific* intention, on a given occasion, to refer to a certain object" (p. 264, his italics). This is where the account bogs down. In the sense in which I really do have both general and specific intentions (e.g. I have a specific intention to drive to Berkeley tomorrow, and a general intention to drive on the right hand side of the road, ceteris paribus, whenever I drive in the United States) I have no such general intentions about definite descriptions. If my use of definite descriptions required such general intentions I would have to form an infinite number of them since there are an infinite number of definite descriptions I am able to use and understand in my language. Consider the definite description (without indexicals), "The man eating a ham sandwich on the top of the Empire State Building at 10 a.m., June 17, 1953." Kripke tells us that in my idiolect the semantic referent of this designator is given by my general intention to refer to a certain object whenever the designator is used. I can only say that I never formed and do not have any such general intention, and I venture to guess that you haven't either. I know what the expression means, and in so knowing I know under what conditions it would be correct to use this expression with a specific intention to perform the speech act of reference with it. That is, I know what conditions an object would have to satisfy in order that I could refer to that object as satisfying the aspects expressed in the definite descriptions. But in addition to knowing the meaning and having specific intentions on specific occasions I don't have any general intentions of the sort Kripke describes. And even supposing I did form a general intention for this case, it would be no help because there would still be literally an infinity of other cases for which I have no such general intentions. Suppose I decided to use this expression only to refer to Jones. Then in my idiolect I would indeed have a general intention which I could express by saying: "I have a general intention to refer to Jones whenever I use the expression 'the man eating a ham sandwich on top of the Empire State Building at 10 a.m., June 17, 1953'" but that still leaves me with an infinite number of other definite descriptions for which I do not have any such general intentions. Furthermore, I don't need any such general intentions to account for my use of definite descriptions. I know the meanings of the elements of the language and the rules of their combination into larger expressions. This knowledge enables me to figure out what aspects are expressed by any new definite description I hear or form, and this knowledge I then use when I utter specific definite descriptions with specific intentions to refer to specific objects on specific occasions. What additional jobs are general intentions supposed to do? Perhaps because Kripke tries to account for Donnellan's alleged distinction in terms of what I believe is a mistaken theory of "general intentions", he fails to see that the real distinction is between primary and secondary aspects under which reference is made.

4. De re *and* de dicto

Many philosophers believe the referential–attributive distinction is somehow closely related to, perhaps even identical with, the *de re–de dicto* distinction. I think both distinctions are for the most part bogus. But it is instructive to see why people have believed there were such distinctions (i.e. to see what real distinctions give rise to the beliefs in these distinctions) and to see why they thought the two alleged distinctions were related or the same. I hope I have made my doubts about referential and attributive clear. My discussion of the *de dicto–de re* distinction will be much briefer; I will not try to state the whole argument, and my remarks will apply only to the distinction as it is supposed to apply to intentional states, such as belief and desire, and to speech acts and to those only as they contain references to particulars. I will, in short, not be concerned with the *de re–de dicto* distinction as it applies to modal contexts or concerns references to abstract entities, such as numbers.

I believe that the theory that there is a distinction between *de re* and *de dicto* beliefs (for example) arises from a confusion between features of reports of beliefs and features of the beliefs being reported. If I know that Ralph believes that the man he saw in the brown hat is a spy, and I also know that the man in the brown hat is B. J. Ortcutt I might report his belief by saying either, "About Ortcutt, Ralph believes he is a spy" or "Ralph believes that the man he saw in the brown hat is a spy."[4] The first of these reports commits me, the reporter, to the existence of an object satisfying the referential content of Ralph's belief, the second does not; and we might call these *de re reports* and *de dicto reports* respectively. But it simply does not follow from the fact that there are two different ways of *reporting* a belief that there are two different *kinds* of belief being reported. Ralph's belief is the same in the two cases. The difference is only in how much I, the reporter, care to commit myself about how much of the truth conditions of his belief are in fact satisfied. The *de re–de dicto* distinction is in short a distinction between ways of reporting beliefs not between different kinds of beliefs.

The simplest way to see this is to see that the distinction which I, the reporter, can make in reporting Ralph's beliefs is not one he can make when he has or gives expression to his beliefs. Suppose he says either, "About the man I saw in the brown hat, I believe he is a spy" or "I believe the man I saw in the brown hat is a spy." From his point of view there is no way he can distinguish between them. Though in the surface syntax "the man in the brown hat" lies outside the scope of "believe" in one case and not in the other, in fact the whole of both sentences gives expression to the same content of Ralph's belief. This is even more obvious in the case of statements. Consider the statements made by Ralph in utterances of

"The man I saw in the brown hat is a spy"

and

"About the man I saw in the brown hat, he is a spy."

The truth conditions are exactly the same in each case. The reason the reporter can make a distinction that Ralph cannot make is that the reporter can decide how much of Ralph's belief he is going merely to report and how much he is going to commit himself to. In a *de dicto* report he reports the entire

---

[4] The example is of course from Quine (1956).

content of the belief and does not commit himself to the existence of an object the belief is ostensibly about. In the *de re* report, of the sort we gave above, he reports only a fragment of the belief, expressed by "is a spy", and commits himself to the existence of an object that the belief was ostensibly about, though not necessarily under the same aspect as Ralph. But Ralph is committed to the whole thing under his own aspects; that is what makes it his belief or his statement.

A great deal of effort has been wasted on the question: when does a report of a speech act or mental state entail the existence of an object that the state or act is about, when is "exportation" a valid form of inference? The answer is: If we are just reporting the content of the belief or act, what the man believes or says, it is never valid. How could it be? From the fact that a man has a certain belief or made a certain statement nothing follows about how much of the truth conditions of his belief or statement are satisfied. One might as well ask, "When does the report of a man's belief entail that the belief is true?" In both cases one can only answer: reporting that a man has a belief with a certain content is one thing, reporting how much of it is true is something else. Reports of the first kind never entail reports of the second kind.

In addition to the distinction between *de dicto* and *de re* reports, there is, furthermore, a genuine distinction between general beliefs and specific beliefs as exemplified by the beliefs Ralph would express if he said respectively, "There are spies (spies exist)" and "The man in the brown hat is a spy." But this is a separate distinction independent of the distinction between *de dicto* and *de re* reports of specific beliefs.

We can now see the relations between the *de re* – *de dicto* distinction and the referential–attributive distinction: as standardly described in the literature, neither distinction exists. There are however some other distinctions that do exist and give rise to the illusory belief in these two distinctions; there is a distinction between reference under primary and secondary aspects and a distinction between reports of beliefs and of speech acts that commit the reporter to the existence of an object referred to and those that do not.

The connection between primary and secondary reference and *de dicto* and *de re* reports is that we are more likely to make *de re* reports of secondary aspect references and more likely to make *de dicto* reports of primary aspect references. Why? Because in the report of a secondary aspect reference we know that the actual aspect expressed in the speaker's utterance was not crucial to the statement he was making and we know that he had other aspects under which he could have made the reference. In the report of a statement where reference is made explicitly under the primary aspect the report will leave out something crucial to the content of the statement if we do not report the primary aspect.

However, as we saw above in our discussion of Donnellan's condition 4, these are only tendencies and there can also be *de re* reports of primary aspect references and there can be *de dicto* reports of secondary aspect references (in the old jargon, this would amount to saying that attributive beliefs can be *de re* and referential beliefs can be *de dicto*, though I hasten to repeat that this way of expressing it is one I reject). Thus if I know the sheriff said "attributively", "Smith's murderer is insane", and I know Jones is Smith's murderer I might indeed tell Jones, "Jones, the sheriff believes you are insane", or even report, "About Jones, the sheriff believes he is insane." Furthermore even where I know that Jones is not Smith's murderer and I know that Ralph said referentially "Smith's murderer is insane", and I know he had Jones in mind, I can still report his speech act by saying, "Ralph said that Smith's murderer is insane", for he did indeed say just that. Both reports, though true, are misleading, for a hearer might reasonably take me to imply by the first that the sheriff said of Jones *under the aspect "Jones"* that he was insane, and he didn't say that, he only said it of him under the aspect "Smith's murderer"; and the second might be taken to imply that the man Ralph had in mind was in fact Smith's murderer, when it wasn't. It was Jones.

Notice incidentally that if the sheriff says, in giving examples of tautologies, "Smith's murderer is Smith's murderer" and "the smallest spy is a spy", even if we know that Jones is Smith's murderer and Boris is the smallest spy

we can't say to Jones, "The sheriff says you are the murderer"
and to Boris, "The sheriff says you are a spy." Why not?
Because in order that the sheriff be saying something about
some object he referred to, it must be the case that what he says
differs from the aspect under which he makes the reference;
otherwise, there is no content to what is said other than that
content which makes it about that which it is said.

5. Russell and Strawson

This whole dispute about Referential and Attributive grew
out of the controversy between Russell and Strawson on the
analysis of definite descriptions. Donnellan claims that both
neglect the referential use and that in consequence there are
serious weaknesses in both of their accounts. If I am right in
my analysis, their accounts and the dispute between them
remains untouched by Donnellan's arguments. Their
accounts are properly construed as about cases in which there
is no secondary aspect, where what the speaker means
coincides with what he says. The fact that there are cases
where the speaker means more than what he says, cases where
the sentence he utters expresses a secondary aspect under
which reference is made but does not express the primary
aspect which counts in the truth conditions of the statement,
is really quite irrelevant to the dispute between Russell and
Strawson, since in such cases there will be some (actual or
possible) sentence which expresses the statement that the
speaker is making and that sentence will be subject to either
the Russellian or the Strawsonian analysis.

Chapter 7

SPEECH ACTS AND RECENT
LINGUISTICS

Until fairly recently it seemed possible to draw a boundary, however vague, between linguistics and the philosophy of language: linguistics dealt with the empirical facts of natural human languages; the philosophy of language dealt with the conceptual truths that underlie any possible language or system of communication. Within the terms of this distinction, the study of speech acts seemed to lie clearly on the side of the philosophy of language, and until the past few years most of the research on speech acts was done by philosophers and not by linguists. Lately, however, all this has changed. In the current period of expansion, linguists have simply moved into large territories where previously only philosophers worked, and the writings of such philosophers as Austin, Grice, and others have now been assimilated into the working tools of the contemporary linguist. The philosopher of language can only welcome this development, for the linguist brings to bear a knowledge of the facts of natural human languages, together with techniques of syntactical analysis which, at least in the past, have been absent from the purely philosophical writings on language. The collaboration between linguists and philosophers is especially fruitful in studying what to me is one of the most interesting questions in the study of language: how do structure and function interact? This question involves such questions as, for example, what is the relation between the various kinds of illocutionary acts and the syntactical forms in which they are realized in the various natural human languages?

However, not all of the contributions of linguists to the study of speech acts have been equally useful, and in this chapter I want to discuss two well-known approaches, both of which seem to me to be mistaken. They are the so-called performative deletion analysis, deriving from the work of John R. Ross (especially his article, "On Declarative Sentences", Ross, 1970) and the conversational postulates approach to the study of indirect speech acts, the best-known exposition of which is in an article by David Gordon and George Lakoff entitled, "Conversational Postulates" (1971). Both of these theories seem to me to be mistaken explanations of the data concerning speech acts, and both – though in their quite different ways – make the same mistake of postulating a much too powerful explanation to account for certain facts, when there already exists an independently motivated theory of speech acts that will account for these facts.

Let me say before I start that it is quite possible that none of the authors I will be discussing still accepts the theses they advanced in these articles. I am not, however, interested in the biographies of these linguists, but rather in certain patterns of analysis that they have advanced. These patterns of analysis have proved influential, as a look at some of the linguistic literature will show, and it is important, I believe, to refute them, regardless of whether their original authors still adhere to them.

I

I begin with Ross's (1970) article. The thesis of this paper, Ross says, "is that declarative sentences, such as those in (1) ['Prices slumped.'] must be analysed as being implicit performatives, and must be derived from deep structures containing an explicitly represented performative main verb" (p. 223). Ross then gives us fourteen syntactic arguments to show that every declarative sentence must have a higher subject "I", must have an indirect object "you" and must have some performative verb, possibly abstract, as the main verb of the highest clause. The conclusion of his discussion then is that every declarative sentence of English has a deep structure of the form, "I say to you that S" or "I tell you that S", etc. Furthermore, it is easy to extend the types of arguments he presents to other sorts of sentences, and the conclusion that is eventually reached (though he does not state it in his original article) is that all English sentences have a performative main verb in the highest clause of their deep structure. A spectacular conclusion. As the arguments in his original article seem to me to exhibit a common inferential pattern, I will consider only the first. If we consider examples like (all of these examples are from Ross's paper):

1. Tom believed that the paper had been written by Ann and him himself

2. Tom believed that the paper had been written by Ann and himself

3. *Tom believed that the paper had been written by Ann and themselves.

These (and many other examples) naturally lead us to the following rule formulation:

4. If an anaphoric pronoun precedes an emphatic reflexive, the former may be deleted, if it is commanded by the NP with which it stands in an anaphoric relationship.

He then goes on to consider examples like:

5. This paper was written by Ann and myself.

Furthermore, he then goes on to give a whole sequence of sentences on the model of 1 and on the model of 5, of which he says that "the acceptability spectra" match each other, exactly or nearly so. But if 4 is really a valid rule, and the examples certainly suggest it is, then in order to account for 5 we have to assume that its deep structure "will contain a higher performative clause which is obliterated by the rule of performative deletion, after the application of the rule stated in (4)" (p. 228). Furthermore, he adds that whether or not the performative analysis is correct, all of these examples must be accounted for by the same rules or principles.

I must say that I find Ross's arguments very subtle and elegant. But what exactly is their logical form? They appear to be of the same logical form as some of the very early arguments used to prove the existence of a syntactic deep structure. For example, consider the sequence:

6. Hit him
7. *Hit you
8. Hit yourself
9. *She hit himself
10. He hit himself
11. You hit yourself
12. *He hit yourself.

In these early discussions of syntactical deep structure it was claimed that in order to account for the occurrence of reflexives in imperative sentences, one has to postulate the occurrence of a second person pronoun "you" in the deep structure of all imperative sentences; in order that the same rule should account for the distribution of reflexives over declarative and imperative sentences. But again, what exactly is the logical form of these arguments?

It seems to be this: for any language L and any two forms F and G, if F and G generally occur together in the surface structure of sentences, and if facts about the form or presence of one are determined by the nature of the other, then for any sentence S in which F occurs in the surface structure, but G does not occur, there is some deep structure of S in which G occurs, but where it is deleted in the surface structure.

Now as a general argument form that is certainly not valid; that is, it simply does not follow from the fact that F and G generally occur together and are related in certain ways in the surface structure that where one is absent, the other must exist in the deep structure. I don't suppose any linguist ever thought that it did follow logically, but nonetheless, this has been an extremely influential pattern of argument. Why? The pattern of inference, we are told, enables us to give a *simpler* account of the data. We require only one rule for the distribution of reflexives, whereas otherwise, if we did not postulate the occurrence of some element in the deep structure, we would require two rules. It is this appeal to an intuitive notion of simplicity that has made the inference pattern so attractive, but I believe the appearance of simplicity rests on an unexamined assumption, which I would like to challenge in the course of this chapter.

The assumption is that *the rules which specify the distribution of syntactical elements must mention only syntactical categories.*

It may seem puzzling to accuse linguists who are famous for denying the autonomy of syntax of assuming such a principle, but unless they assume it, it is hard to see how they justify their acceptance of the performative deletion analysis or of the traditional (and, I believe, confused) arguments to show that imperative sentences have a deleted second person subject.

Before going on to challenge this assumption, I want to mention a couple of other arguments that were not in Ross's original article but which have subsequently been used to justify the performative analysis: consider sentences like:

13. Frankly, you're drunk.

"Frankly" in 13 does not seem to function as a sentence adverb as does "probably" in

14. Probably, it will rain.

Both syntactically and semantically, it has been argued, 13 requires us to postulate an underlying verb of saying in the deep structure. This is because, syntactically, "frankly" normally co-occurs with verbs of saying as in

15. John frankly admitted his guilt

but not with other sorts of verbs, as in, e.g.,

16. *It frankly rained

and semantically, because there is nothing for "frankly" to modify in the surface structure of 13. The verb it modifies must be something other than what is in its surface structure. Therefore, the deep structure of 13, so the argument goes, must be the same as that of sentences of the form:

17. I verb you frankly: you're drunk.

Another class of arguments for performative deletion analysis concern adverbial clauses. For example,

18. Since you know so much, why did John leave?

And here, it is argued, in order to account for the occurrence of the adverbial clause one has to postulate a deep structure similar to that of

19. Since you know so much, I ask you (am asking you) why did John leave?

These and many other arguments all lead to the same conclusion. Every sentence of English and presumably of every other language has a performative main verb in its deep structure. These arguments have been attacked in their details by various authors, but I believe that so far no one has challenged the fundamental assumptions on which these arguments rest. Before doing that, I want to call attention to what an intuitively implausible conclusion the performative deletion analysis leads to. It has the consequence that in an important sense of "saying" you can only perform an illocutionary act by saying that you are performing it, for the deep structure of every sentence you utter contains "an explicitly represented performative main verb". I find it hard to imagine that any arguments of the sort we have considered could convince one of such a counterintuitive conclusion.

I believe there is a much simpler explanation of the data, and the explanation contains only the assumption of elements which are "independently motivated" by the theory of speech acts. Ross almost considers this explanation, but he does not quite face it squarely. It is this:

In any speech situation there is a speaker, a hearer and a speech act being performed by the speaker. The speaker and the hearer share a mutual knowledge of those facts together with a mutual knowledge of the rules of performing the various kinds of speech acts. These facts and this knowledge enable us to account for certain syntactical forms without forcing us to assume that the facts themselves have some syntactical description or representation in the deep structure of sentences that they help to explain. For example, in 13, "frankly" is predicated of the speech act that is being performed in the utterance of the sentence. It is not necessary to assume that it also modifies a verb, rather it characterizes the act which the speaker is performing, and that act need not be and in this case is not represented by a verb anywhere in the deep structure of the sentence, since the speaker and hearer already have mutual knowledge of the existence of that act. In the utterance of 18 we see the same phenomena at work. The speaker asks a question and in so doing gives a reason for asking it. This explanation is quite adequate without any further requirement that there must be some verb of asking which the adverbial clause modifies. This sort of phenomenon, where the speaker conjoins the performance of a speech act with the giving of a reason for performing it, in the utterance of one and the same sentence, is very common in English. Consider:

20. He must be home by now, because I saw him on his way half an hour ago.

Here the "because" clause does not give a reason or a cause for its being the case that he is home; my seeing him does not cause him to be home by now; rather, it gives a justification for my *saying* that he must be at home, by giving the evidentiary basis for my saying and believing it.

Ross almost considers this approach but not quite. He considers what he calls "the pragmatic analysis". This analysis, says Ross, "claims that certain elements are present in the context of a speech act and that syntactic processes can refer to such elements". The context provides an "I", a "you", and a performative verb which are " 'in the air' so to speak" (Ross, 1970, p. 254 ff). It is crucial to Ross's characterization of the pragmatic analysis that it postulates the presence not of speakers, hearers, and acts but of the words, "I", "you", and the performative verbs. But given that the pragmatic analysis postulates the presence of words, it would seem to differ only very slightly from the performative deletion analysis which Ross subscribes to; and indeed, he says, "Given this isomorphism [of the performative and pragmatic analyses], it may well be asked how the pragmatic analysis differs from the performative analysis: why are they not merely notational variants?" I believe that as he presents the two they are just notational variants of each other, but for that very reason he has missed the point of talking about the "context" in which the speech act is performed: the speaker, the hearer and the speech act performed by the speaker are not in the air; they are very much on the ground. The "elements" in the analysis I am presenting are not the words "I", "you" and the performative verbs, but speakers, hearers, and acts performed by speakers. It is only if one accepts the so far unjustified and unargued assumption that syntactical rules can only make mention of syntactical categories that one would ever want to construct a "pragmatic analysis" of the sort Ross considers. What I am arguing is that there is no need to postulate an "I", a "you", or a verb either in the air or in the deep structure, once that assumption is abandoned, since we already have an independent motivation for believing that in speech situations there are speakers, hearers and speech acts, and it is these elements which are referred to in the statement of the relevant syntactic rules. It has been suggested to me (by David Reier) that perhaps Ross makes this confusion because he is committing a use–mention fallacy; that is, he is confusing the speaker and the "I" which refers to him, the hearer and the "you" which refers to him, and the acts and the verbs which specify those acts. Of course, the formulation of the rules which mention speaker, hearer and act will *use* expressions to refer to speaker, hearer and act, but it will use and not mention those expressions. Under the analysis I am proposing, the statement of the rule will contain, for example, the use of an illocutionary verb, but it would be a simple use–mention confusion of the most egregious variety to suppose that the rule mentions (or refers to or is about) a verb. I find it hard to believe that Ross is guilty of so elementary a mistake, rather it seems more plausible to assume that he is in the grip of the assumption that if the rules are to be adequate they must mention only syntactic elements. And that, I believe, is why when he presents the "pragmatic analysis" it is not a pragmatic analysis at all but a variant syntactical analysis.

But isn't the performative deletion analysis and the deleted subject analysis of imperatives simpler in some fairly clear sense of simpler than the alternative I have been proposing? I

169

think these theories fail the test of simplicity provided by Occam's razor: a theory should not postulate the existence of more entities than is necessary to account for the facts. Since we already know that a speech situation contains a hearer, a speaker, and a speech act, it is an unnecessary complexity to introduce deleted syntactical elements corresponding to these entities. It appears simpler only if we insist on the principle that syntactical rules can mention only syntactical categories. Once we abandon this assumption, our alternative theory becomes simpler in two respects. First, we use independently motivated semantic and "pragmatic" knowledge; and, secondly, we do not have to postulate any deleted syntactical elements. Consider how this would work for imperative sentences. There is an independently motivated propositional content rule on the directive class of speech acts to the effect that the propositional content of a directive predicates some future course of action of the hearer (see Searle, 1969, p. 66). Now since in English the imperative form is the standard illocutionary-force-indicating device for directives, the literal utterance of an imperative form necessarily involves a predication of the hearer. It is therefore not necessary to assume an additional syntactical representation of the hearer. Reference to the hearer is already contained in the relevant rules of speech acts. The reflexive rule does indeed involve a repeated element, but that element need not always be present in the syntax. In

He hit himself

the repetition that permits the reflexive is present in the syntax because the subject and object are coreferential; but in

Hit yourself

there is no repetition in the syntax, because there does not need to be. It follows from the theory of speech acts that in the utterance of this sentence the verb "hit" is predicated of the hearer. But it does not follow from that fact that the sentence has a syntactical subject "you". Rather, the sentence does not have a syntactical subject, because, being an English imperative, it doesn't need one. Of course, not all languages are like English in this regard. The point is not that the theory of speech acts forces the elimination of the subject expression in imperative sentences, but rather that the theory explains the possibility of that elimination.

I think that the forms of the argument we have been considering are not valid or even intuitively plausible forms of inference. I think that they have seemed appealing because of certain tacit assumptions about what syntactical rules should look like. As a further indication that something is fishy about the form of the argument, I want to call your attention to some counterintuitive results that a consistent adherence to the argument form would produce. Consider nonimperative sentences that can take a preverbal "please", e.g.

21. Can you please pass the salt? or
22. Will you please leave us alone?

Now since "please" normally occurs with the imperative mood as in

23. Please pass the salt

I suppose a consistent adherence to the Ross argument form would force us to say that each of these sentences has an imperative deep structure, and, consequently, that sentences of the form

24. Can you plus vol verb

and

25. Will you plus vol verb

are really ambiguous, as they have both an imperative and a declarative deep structure. This seems to me a most implausible result, especially since there is a very simple explanation of the occurrence of "please" in nonimperative sentences like the above: these sentences are often used to perform indirect requests, and "please" makes the request more polite. It can be inserted before the verb which names the act being requested. A similar reductio ad absurdum argument can be constructed for sentences containing an anaphoric pronoun with no NP antecedent. In a sentence such as

26. He's drunk

are we really to say that there is a deep structure NP that is an antecedent to "He"? It would seem that a consistent adherence to the traditional argument forms would force us to that conclusion.

Let me conclude this half of the chapter by distinguishing what I am saying from what I am not saying. I am not saying that there are no good arguments for deleted syntactical elements in the deep structure of sentences. A sentence such as

27. I met a richer man than Rockefeller

clearly seems to derive its ambiguity from the fact that there are two different possible deleted elements corresponding to

28. I met a richer man than Rockefeller met
29. I met a richer man than Rockefeller is.

It is because of these two deletions that we can use 27 to say two quite different things represented by 28 and 29. But in that sense of "say", when I say that prices slumped, I am not also saying that I am saying it. It is an intuitively implausible result to suppose that I can only perform an illocutionary act by using a sentence with an explicit performative verb in its deep structure, and the arguments that might incline one to this result are easily accounted for by a theory of speech acts which we already have some reason to believe is true.

II

I now turn to the second half of this chapter, the discussion of the conversational postulates approach to the study of indirect speech acts, the most well-known version of which is in the article by Gordon and Lakoff. For the sake of brevity, I will discuss their article under the following headings. (1) What is the problem? (2) What is their solution? (3) Why is it inadequate? and finally, (4) I will try to suggest an alternative approach from the point of view of the theory of speech acts. To anticipate a bit, my general criticism of their approach will be that they offer the phenomena that need to be explained as if they were themselves the explanation.

The problem is simply this. How is it possible for the speaker to say one thing, mean what he says, but also to mean something else. I say

30. Can you reach the salt?

or

31. I would appreciate it if you would get off my foot

but I mean not only what I say but also I mean: *pass the salt*, and *get off my foot*. In such cases the primary illocutionary point of the utterance is that of a request to do something, but the literal and secondary illocutionary point is that of a question or statement. How is it possible for the speaker to mean the non-literal primary illocutionary point and for the hearer to understand the non-literal primary illocutionary point when all the speaker utters is a sentence expressing the literal secondary illocutionary point? A second aspect of the problem is this. Many of the sentences that are most commonly used in the performances of indirect speech acts seem to be systematically related to the primary illocutionary point that they are indirectly used to convey. Thus, for example, consider the sequence of sentences that concern the hearer's ability to perform the action.

Can you pass the salt?
Could you pass the salt?
Are you able to reach that book on the top shelf?
You can go now
You could get off my foot.

All of these have a very natural use as indirect requests and some of them will take "please". Furthermore, they seem to be systematically related to one of the preparatory rules on the performance of the directive class of illocutionary acts, the rule that says that the hearer must be able to perform the act and that the speaker and hearer must believe that he is so able. Or consider the sequence of sentences such as

I would like you to go now
I want you to leave the room
I would appreciate it if you would get off my foot
I should be most grateful if you could take off your hat.

All such examples concern the speaker's desire that the hearer do something; and, in a theory of speech acts, the speaker's desire or want that the hearer should do an action is the sincerity condition on the directive class of speech acts. A third set of examples is provided by sentences such as

Will you leave the room?
Would you kindly go now?
Are you going to continue to make so much noise?

and so on. All of these again relate to a condition on speech acts, namely, the propositional content condition that the speaker predicates a future course of action of the hearer. So we have both a general problem of accounting for the move from literal to primary illocutionary points and, within that problem, there is a special problem of accounting for the fact that certain sets of sentences seem to be systematically related both to indirect speech acts and to our general theory of speech acts.[1] How should we account for these problems?

The solution that Gordon and Lakoff (1971) propose is really quite simple. They claim that in addition to the rules such as those above for the performance of directive speech acts (the preparatory, sincerity, and propositional content rules), the speaker knows an additional set of rules called conversational postulates: and "it is by means of such postulates that we can get one speech act to entail another speech act". Thus, for example, the conversational postulate

$$\text{ASK } (a,b, \text{ CAN } (b,Q))^* \to \text{REQUEST } (a,b,Q)$$

tells us that if *a* asks *b* a defective question as to whether *b* can do the act specified in *Q*, then that question "entails"[2] a request from *a* to *b* to do that act. That is, these

---

[1] A third problem is that in some sentences, e.g., "Are you going to continue to make so much noise?" the indirect request negates the propositional content.

[2] Literally it makes no sense to speak of one *act* entailing another act. Entailment is a relation between propositions, not between acts, whether speech acts or otherwise.

conversational postulates are supposed to be additional rules that the speaker–hearer knows which enable him to go through the alleged "entailments".

What exactly is the form of their solution to the problem? It seems to me that the form is something like this. They have described a fairly well-known pattern of indirect speech acts, at least within the directive class. They then suppose that the patterns are themselves the solution, for the conversational postulates that they use to explain the data derive directly from the patterns. That is, they discover a pattern to the effect that a speaker can ask a hearer to do something by asking the hearer if he is able to do it. In order to account for this, they simply redescribe it by saying that the speaker knows a rule, or rather, conversational postulate, to the effect that if you ask a hearer a (defective) question about his ability to do something, the utterance is ("entails") a request to him to do it. Furthermore, the mistake seems to me quite similar in form to the mistake that I am alleging against Ross. In both cases, an unnecessary supposition is made in order to account for the data. In this case we already have a theory of conversation of the Gricean type; and we have a theory of illocutionary acts of a sort outlined in *Speech Acts*, and we know certain things about speakers' and hearers' powers of inference and rationality. It is entirely ad hoc and unmotivated to claim that, in addition to all of this knowledge, the speaker–hearer must have some extra knowledge of a set of conversational postulates. The hypostatization, in short, of conversational postulates seems to me to be unnecessary and unsupported by the evidence and, indeed, the phenomena recorded by the postulates are precisely what we need to explain. They do not themselves provide the explanation.

I think these objections will become clearer if we remind ourselves of the alternative account of indirect speech acts presented in chapter 2 of this volume (Searle 1975b). Consider the simplest sort of case: someone at a dinner table says to me

Can you pass the salt?

Now it is quite clear that unless the circumstances are most peculiar he is not just asking me whether I can pass the salt; he is asking me to pass him the salt.

Sure I can pass the salt

is not by itself an adequate answer. Now, how do I know that? How do I get from the knowledge that he has asked me whether I can pass the salt to the knowledge that he has asked me to pass him the salt? And that question, how do I understand the primary illocutionary act when all he says is the secondary illocutionary act?, is part of the answer to the question: how is it possible for him to *mean* the primary illocutionary act when all that he actually says is the secondary illocutionary act. Two answers I am rejecting are: first, that the sentence is ambiguous, that it really has two different meanings, and, secondly, that I must know an extra rule or conversational postulate to the effect that whenever somebody asks me a certain sort of question about whether I can do something, he is really asking me to do it. I think, indeed, that, as a generalization, it is largely correct; that is, in our culture whenever somebody asks you certain sorts of questions, they are usually trying to get you to do something, but it is that generalization which our theory needs to explain; the mistake is to suppose that we have explained it or anything else by calling the generalization a "conversational postulate".

I will not here set out the steps necessary for the hearer to derive the primary indirect illocution from the literal secondary illocution since they are stated in some detail in chapter 2. The apparatus necessary for the hearer to make the inference includes a theory of speech acts, a theory of conversation, factual background information, and general powers of rationality and inference. Each of these is independently motivated, that is, we have evidence quite independent of any theory of indirect speech acts that the speaker–hearer has these features of linguistic and cognitive competence. And the hypothesis being put forth in that chapter is that all the cases can be analyzed using this apparatus, without involving any "conversational postulates".

We might summarize the difference between this approach

and the conversational postulates approach as follows: Both agree that there are sets of generalizations that one can make about indirect speech acts, for example, generalizations such as that one can make an indirect request to a hearer to do something by asking him if he is able to do it. On my account these generalizations are to be explained by a theory of speech acts, including a theory of conversation, and by the assumption that speakers and hearers know certain general things about the world and have certain general powers of rationality. On the conversational postulates approach, each generalization is elevated to the status of a rule or conversational postulate, and we are asked to suppose that people understand indirect speech acts because they know these rules ("it is by means of such postulates that we can get one speech act to entail another speech act"). On my account there is no reason to believe in the existence of any such rules, because our existing theories will already account for the existence of indirect speech acts, and indeed, the rules have no explanatory power since they are mere reformulations of the material we need to explain.

Incidentally, the actual rules that they propose don't work. Consider, for example, the one just mentioned. Stripped of its "formalization", it says that whenever you ask somebody a defective question about whether he can do something, you are asking him to do that thing. By "defective" they mean that the question is not intended to be conveyed, and the hearer assumes it is not intended to be conveyed. But such a claim is, I believe, simply false. Thus, if I say

Can you eat the square root of Mount Everest?

I have certainly asked a defective question in their sense because I know that the final noun phrase contains a category mistake and hence I do not intend to convey a genuine question, and I assume you know that. But it simply does not follow from this, nor is it the case that, my utterance conveys, implies, or "entails" a request. Such counterexamples will work for all of their conversational postulates. It is also worth noting that the actual cases of successful indirect speech acts are in general cases where the literal secondary illocution is conveyed, and the primary illocutionary act is successful only because the secondary illocutionary act is conveyed.

I now want to draw some general conclusions from the discussion of these two patterns of analysis. Both of them seem to me to exhibit a mistaken conception of the place of a theory of speech acts within a general account of language. It is common to hear people say, following Chomsky, that the task of linguistics is to specify the set of rules that relate sound and meanings. Each language provides a set, presumably infinite, of possible sound sequences and another set, presumably infinite, of possible meanings. The phonological, syntactical, and semantic components of the grammar are supposed to provide the finite sets of rules which the speaker knows and which enable him to go from sound to meaning and back again. I don't think that this picture is false, so much as it is extremely misleading and misleading in ways which have had unfortunate consequences for research. A more accurate picture seems to me this. The purpose of language is communication. The unit of human communication in language is the speech act, of the type called illocutionary act. The problem (or at least one important problem) of the theory of language is to describe how we get from the sounds to the illocutionary acts. What, so to speak, has to be added to the noises that come out of my mouth in order that their production should be a performance of the act of asking a question, or making a statement, or giving an order, etc. The rules enable us to get from the brute facts of the making of noises to the institutional facts of the performance of illocutionary acts of human communication. Now, if that is the case, then the role of a theory of speech acts in a grammar will be quite different from what either the proponents of generative syntax or even most of the proponents of generative semantics have considered. The theory of speech acts is not an adjunct to our theory of language, something to be consigned to the realm of "pragmatics", or performance; rather, the theory of speech acts will necessarily occupy a central role in our grammar, since it will include all of what used to be called semantics as well as pragmatics.

Furthermore, the theory will provide us with a set of rules for performing illocutionary acts, which rules may have consequences in other parts of our linguistic theory, such as syntax. It is not at all surprising that the theory of speech acts should have syntactical consequences, since, after all, that is what sentences are for. A sentence is to talk with. My objection to the two theories I have discussed in this chapter is that they both fail to use the resources of existing theories of speech acts. Both, when confronted with puzzling data, postulate a solution which requires the introduction of extra and unnecessary elements. In each, a proper understanding of the role of speech acts would enable us to account for the data without introducing these extra elements.

BIBLIOGRAPHY

G.E.M. Anscombe (1957), *Intentions*, Blackwell.

Aristotle, *Rhetoric and Poetics*.

Asch (1958), "The metaphor: a psychological inquiry", *Person, Perception and Interpersonal Behavior*, Tagiori and Petrullo (eds.), Stanford University Press.

J. L. Austin (1962), *How to Do Things With Words*, J. O. Urmson (ed.), Oxford, Clarendon Press.

M. C. Beardsley (1962), "The metaphorical twist", *Philosophy and Phenomenological Research*, Vol. 22.

M. Black (1962), "Metaphor". In M. Black, *Models and Metaphors*.

– (1979), "More about metaphor", *Metaphor and Thought*, Andrew Ortony (ed.), Cambridge University Press.

S. Cavell (1976), *Must We Mean What We Say?*, Cambridge University Press.

Keith S. Donnellan (1966), "Reference and Definite Descriptions", *Philosophical Review*, Vol. 75.

– (1968), "Putting Humpty Dumpty Together Again", *Philosophical Review*, Vol. 77.

David Gordon and George Lakoff (1971), "Conversational Postulates", *Papers from the Seventh Regional Meeting of the Chicago Linguistic Society*, Chicago.

H. Paul Grice (1975), "Logic and Conversation", *Syntax and Semantics, Vol. 3, Speech Acts*, Peter Cole and Jerry L. Morgan (eds.), Academic Press.

Paul Henle (ed.) (1965), *Language, Thought and Culture*, U. of Mich. Press.

David Holdcroft (1978), *Words and Deeds*, Clarendon Press, Oxford.

Saul Kripke (1977), "Speaker's Reference and Semantic Reference", *Midwest Studies in Philosophy*, Vol. 2.

G. Miller (1979), "Images and models, similes and metaphors", *Metaphor and Thought*, Andrew Ortony (ed.), Cambridge University Press.

W. V. Quine (1956), "Quantifiers and Propositional Attitudes", *Journal of Philosophy*, Vol. 53.

I. A. Richards (1936), *The Philosophy of Rhetoric*, Oxford University Press.

J. R. Ross (1970), "On declarative sentences", *Readings in English Transformational Grammar*, R. A. Jacobs and P. S. Rosenbaum (eds.), Ginn & Co., Waltham, Mass.

John R. Searle (1968), "Austin on Locutionary and Illocutionary Acts", *Philosophical Review*, Vol. 57.

Bibliography

- (1969), *Speech Acts*, Cambridge University Press.
- (1975a), "A Taxonomy of Illocutionary Acts", *Language, Mind and Knowledge, Minnesota Studies in the Philosophy of Science*, Keith Gunderson (ed.), University of Minnesota Press.
- (1975b), "Indirect Speech Acts", in P. Cole and J. L. Morgan (eds.), *Syntax and Semantics, Vol. 3, Speech Acts*, Academic Press.
- (1975c), "The Logical Status of Fictional Discourse", *New Literary History*, Vol. 6.
- (1975d), "Speech Acts and Recent Linguistics", *Developmental Psycholinguistics and Communication Disorders*, Annals of the New York Academy of Sciences, Vol. 263, Doris Aaronson and R. W. Rieber (eds.).
- (1978), "Literal Meaning", *Erkenntnis*, Vol. 13.
- (1979a), "Metaphor", *Metaphor and Thought*, Andrew Ortony (ed.), Cambridge University Press.
- (1979b), "Referential and Attributive", *The Monist*, Vol. 13.
- Ludwig Wittgenstein (1953), *Philosophical Investigations*, Blackwell, Oxford.

INDEX

Index

Index